Otto von Bismarck and Imperial Germany

PROBLEMS IN EUROPEAN
CIVILIZATION SERIES

Otto von Bismarck and Imperial Germany

A Historical Assessment

Third Edition

Edited and with an introduction by
Theodore S. Hamerow
University of Wisconsin

D. C. HEATH AND COMPANY
Lexington, Massachusetts   Toronto

Address editorial correspondence to:

D. C. Heath and Company
125 Spring Street
Lexington, MA 02173

Acquisitions Editor: James Miller
Managing Editor: Sylvia Mallory
Production Editor: Carolyn Ingalls
Designer: Alwyn Velásquez
Photo Researcher: Billie Ingram
Production Coordinator: Richard Tonachel
Permissions Editor: Margaret Roll

Cover: *The Proclamation of the German Empire.* Anton von Werner, 1885. Friedrichsruher Collection/Bismarck Museum. Archiv für Kunst und Geschichte, Berlin. King Wilhelm I of Prussia is acclaimed as German Emperor in the Hall of Mirrors in the Palace of Versailles, of 18 January 1971.

International Standard Book Number: 0-669-29444-6

Library of Congress Catalog Number: 92-76066

10 9 8 7 6 5 4 3 2 1

Preface

Since the previous edition of this book was published in 1972, historical research on Bismarck has not only grown rapidly but has changed direction as well. Its focus had formerly centered on the man and his statecraft. That is, scholars had tended to stress the formative experiences in Bismarck's life, his transformation from a conservative landowner into a gifted politician, his diplomatic skill in achieving German unification, his strategies and goals as the leading statesman of Europe, and his methods and purposes as the chancellor of the empire he had created. But more recently attention has shifted from the man to the times in which he lived, from politics and diplomacy to economics and society, from warfare to urbanization, from foreign alliances to the growth of industry, and from changes in international relations to changes in the standard of living. In short, a far-reaching alteration in scholarly interest and emphasis has taken place.

I have tried to reflect that alteration in this third edition of the book. My strong feeling is that it would be a mistake to omit entirely the work of those great scholars who had once dominated the arena of Bismarck scholarship. To deal with Germany in the second half of the nineteenth century without talking about the Iron Chancellor would be like putting on a performance of *Hamlet* without the Prince of Denmark. But I have also included selections that mirror the newer insights and perceptions, selections on growth of capitalism in Central Europe, for example, on the reinforcement of an old authoritarian tradition, on the fostering of a new military aggressiveness, and on the agonizing question of whether in some way Bismarck's statecraft foreshadowed and facilitated Hitler's. I hope that I have succeeded in at least suggesting the scope and nature of these more recent scholarly interests.

While working on this book, I incurred a debt of gratitude to a large number of people, some of whom are in all probability not even aware of how much I owe them. There are, to begin with, many friends and colleagues in the historical profession, most of them in the University of Wisconsin, who assisted me with their advice and experience in deciding what to include and what to omit. Then there are the outside consultants who provided information on the needs and interests of the present generation of college students. In particular, I would like to acknowledge the comments of Daniel Borg (Clark University), Donald Niewyk (Southern Methodist University), and Harry Ritter (Western Washington University); their suggestions were invaluable to me in deciding what materials would be most useful in the classroom instruction. And finally, there are the members of the editorial staff of D. C. Heath who helped find suitable illustrations and maps for the book in addition to performing the usual tasks of polishing and improving the text. To them and to all the others I want to express my sincere thanks.

T.S.H.

Contents

VI The Bismarckian Legacy 139

Introduction

The theory that history is determined by the great people of an age has long been out of fashion. Even while Thomas Carlyle was delivering his brilliant lectures *On Heroes, Hero Worship and the Heroic in History* more than a hundred and fifty years ago, there were those in the audience who refused to be swayed by his eloquence; and the general trend of historical thinking since those days has been away from the doctrine of the omnipotent genius. Some of us believe that the destiny of our world is being shaped by ideals like democracy, nationalism, the classless society, or the greatest happiness of the greatest number. Others think that the distribution of material resources and rewards forms the essential character of a civilization. There are those who feel that the ultimate arbiter of human affairs is armed might, the ability to create and use nuclear bombs, robot aircraft, space satellites, nerve gases. A few will even maintain that we are all ultimately in the grip of those irrational and subconscious forces that Sigmund Freud discovered deep in the human psyche. However, believers in the heroic determination of history are few and far between.

Yet in a sense we covertly accept what we publicly deny. People may insist on the primacy of ideology in affairs of state, or on the importance of economic relationships, or on the arbitrament of arms, or on the might of the libido. In practice, though, they behave as if it made a great deal of difference whether Kennedy or Reagan, Brezhnev or Gorbachev, Hitler or Adenauer, Chiang Kai-shek or Mao Tse-tung, decides policy. Apparently personalities are not unimportant after all. What is more, on reflection we would probably have to concede that in times of crisis, the role of the individual becomes particularly significant. Would the Union have been preserved if James Buchanan rather than Abraham Lincoln had been inaugurated as president of the United States in the spring of 1861? Could a disorganized faction of doctrinaire radicals have seized power in Russia in 1917 if Lenin had never taken that trip across Germany in a sealed train? How would the people of England have responded in 1940 if Neville Chamberlain or Lord Halifax had demanded of them blood, sweat, and tears? Willy-nilly, we are forced into a semi-Carlylean position. There is a group of political leaders—consider Napoleon, Cavour, Lincoln, Lenin, Churchill—who exercised a profound political influence on the course of events at some crucial point in history. In a very important respect they are the makers of the world in which we live.

Otto von Bismarck belongs in this company. And yet the signficance of the part he played in public affairs remains a subject of bitter dispute a hundred years after his death. His fellows in the pantheon of statesmen have been consigned to their niches, their strengths and weaknesses engraved in marble for all time. They no longer arouse passion; they are no longer controversial. They have ceased to be flesh and blood; they are now tradition. Today the English are willing to admit that Napoleon was not the incarnation of Satan after all, while the French do not insist that he was the greatest hero since Alexander. Lincoln has become a deity of popular democracy in America; we all see him as he sits in that magnificent sculpture by Daniel Chester French, gazing down upon the world with an inexhaustible compassion. Churchill became apotheosized during his own lifetime, like some Roman emperor of the dying ancient world. No one disputes that Hitler was a man of infinite evil. Even Lenin has now become a saint to dedicated communists, a devil to violent reactionaries, and a leader of great gifts serving questionable ends to those in between.

But Bismarck is a law unto himself. The same controversies that raged around the Iron Chancellor while he was alive continue to trouble his eternal rest. He has been portrayed as both the destroyer of liberty and a compromiser with liberalism. His wars of unification are to some a work of political duplicity, to others an act of historic justice. There are those who see in his diplomacy an attempt to maintain German hegemony; others who consider it proof of his wish to preserve the old Europe. His efforts to crush Catholicism and socialism have been explained as the folly of a ruthless authoritarian—or as the struggle of a wise statesman to subdue the forces of national disruption. The clash of opposing interpretations goes on.

The issues posed by Bismarck's statescraft cannot be reduced to a simple formulation. Was he good or bad, a realist or an idealist? Was he a conservative of the old school or a totalitarian forerunner of National Socialism? Was he a "good European" or an advocate of *Deutschland über alles?* These questions are too shallow, too naive to lead to answers that can contribute significantly to our comprehension. The dimensions of the problem are too great to be measured in such antonymous juxtapositions as "innocent or guilty," "progressive or reactionary," "Christian or Machiavellian." It can even be argued that there really is no such thing as a Bismarck problem, that there are rather several Bismarcks and several problems. A statesman whose career extended over thirty years, who helped maintain royal prerogative against parliamentary claims, who successfully asserted Prussia's demand for power in the face of Austrian opposition, who encompassed the fall of one empire in France and established another in Germany, who waged war against the Vatican as well as against Marxism, who directed the diplomatic fortunes of a continent: such a statesman cannot be categorized under any single rubric. To understand the rich complexity of his achievement we must examine it in a variety of contexts and from several points of view.

This book, therefore, begins with a consideration of those personal qualities and private experiences that helped transform a fire-eating reactionary aristocrat into a discerning and imaginative diplomat. The landed noblemen of Prussia among whom Bismarck grew up were a social class distinguished for neither subtlety nor judgment. Yet the Junker of Schönhausen somehow managed to overcome the limitations imposed by his background. When he first entered politics in his thirties as a delegate to the United Diet of 1847, he was an uncompromising enemy of parliamentary government. Twenty years later he became the author of a constitution that gave the suffrage to every adult male, at a time when even in England most men still could not vote. During the revolution of 1848 he worked tirelessly to frustrate liberal plans for the unification of Germany. On January 18, 1871, he stood proudly in the Hall of Mirrors at Versailles, while the German Empire that he had helped create was being proclaimed. At the time of the Austro-Prussian conflict of 1850, he was all for moderation and monarchical solidarity. By 1859 he had become so violently opposed to the diplomacy of the Hofburg that the authorities in Berlin thought it best to send him into genteel exile in the embassy at St. Petersburg. The conservative friends of his youth, who could still remember him as an ultra of the ultras, observed his change of heart first with surprise, then dismay, and finally resentment, until they broke with him at the moment of his greatest triumph. But Bismarck went on maturing in his view of the world long after most others harden in the rigid mold of everyday life.

Why? How could the harsh, stubborn soil of the Prussian latifundia produce a statesman of such subtlety and perception? Here is the question that has fascinated all of his biographers. The ultimate mystery of Bismarck's personality remains unsolved; it is probably insoluble. But there are partial answers that can enlarge our understanding of the man. Some writers have seen in him above all else a country squire of genius, attached to the soil, close to nature, distrustful of the big city with its disintegrating effect on human loyalty. Hence, his devotion to the traditions of the state; hence, his criticism of the liberal addiction to experiment and innovation. Others have focused on the formative intellectual experiences of his youth: on the tendency toward philosophic skepticism; on the romanticist strain in him; above all, on the Pietistic ethic of his Pomeranian friends. It is also clear that the years Bismarck spent in Frankfurt as Prussian representative at the Diet of the German Confederation were a turning point. He was forced to the conclusion that some form of German unification was inevitable and that it ought to be *kleindeutsch* in form, realized under Hohenzollern auspices to the exclusion of Austrian influence. Finally, the art of biography in the twentieth century cannot escape the influence of the Freudian technique and vocabulary. There are those who try to understand the grown statesman by analyzing his childhood experiences, his relationship to his parents, the emotional atmosphere of the paternal home, his youthful associations with men and women. These diverse interpretations of Bismarck as a man are not mutually inconsistent. They differ in emphasis and point of view, but they are complementary rather than exclusive. If they do not resolve the problem, they at least define and clarify it.

While Bismarck the man interests us from the day of his birth or perhaps even one or two generations before that, Bismarck the statesman becomes important only with his appointment as prime minister of Prussia in 1862. He came to power at a critical moment. For the third time in fifty years, the liberals were trying to introduce parliamentary rule in the Hohenzollern monarchy. They had failed once after 1815, when a political reaction followed the exalted mood of the War of Liberation. They had failed again after 1848, when royalist armies crushed the bright hopes of the revolution. Now they were once more challenging the tradition of monarchical absolutism. The immediate issue in the constitutional conflict was army reform, but on its outcome depended the future of representative government in Germany. If the legislature won the right to control the armed forces through the power of the purse, it could go on to assert its authority over all other functions of government as well. The experience of Great Britain would then be repeated in Central Europe.

But Bismarck succeeded in taming parliament. For four long years he governed in defiance of the chamber and in violation of the constitution, until he finally forced the opposition to accept a settlement on his terms. By defeating Austria in the Seven Weeks' War and consolidating all of Germany north of the Main River, he was able to offer the parliamentarians something that was even more precious to them than their parliamentarianism, a united national state. It was an offer they could not refuse. By a vote of 230 to 75 the legislature adopted a bill of indemnity legalizing all the transgressions for which it had repeatedly condemned the prime minister. The best hope of German liberalism failed, and the results of that historic failure continue to be felt a hundred and fifty years later.

No other aspect of Bismarck's statecraft has been the

subject of as much controversy as his role in undermining parliamentary institutions in Germany. His other accomplishments can be regarded with greater equanimity, since they no longer affect us in any immediate way. The empire he built did not survive him by more than twenty years. His complicated system of diplomatic alliances and alignments began to fall apart almost on the day of his dismissal in 1890. His war against Catholics and Marxists recalls King Canute's ordering the rising tide of the Thames to go back. But the corruption of liberalism, that is a different story. It leads directly to the personal rule of William II, to the dictatorship of the high command during World War I, to the tragedy of the Weimar Republic, to the horror of the Third Reich. It summons us irresistibly to take sides. During his lifetime Bismarck was portrayed by many writers as the great compromiser who sought to maintain a healthy balance between monarchical authority and popular democracy. After all, while he may not have approved of parliamentarian doctrines, neither did he agree with the reactionaries who were urging him to reestablish royal absolutism. In the twentieth century, however, he ceased to be the voice of sweet reason. After the fall of the German Empire in 1918 his partisans and critics alike tended to become more drastic. Those who were out of sympathy with democratic institutions invoked his name to prove that only a heroic leader could save their nation from the self-seeking politicians. And those who deplored the growth of totalitarianism in Central Europe attacked his achievement, partly because it led to the seduction of the liberals, partly because it persuaded the liberals to let themselves be seduced. The differences of opinion remain unresolved.

The diplomatic means that Bismarck used to achieve the unification of Germany are controversial as well, for no sharp distinction can be drawn between his domestic and foreign policies. From the beginning he planned to exploit success in the national struggle in order to prevail in the constitutional conflict. Shortly after his appointment as prime minister, he outlined his program of action with frightening candor: "The great questions of the time are not decided by speeches and majority resolutions—that was the big mistake of 1848 and 1849—but by iron and blood." Armed force was for him always an essential element in the relations among governments; he never hesitated to use it where the stakes were high enough. And what stakes could be higher than the establishment of a united German state under the hegemony of Prussia? Not only would patriotic aspirations be realized through the leadership of the Hohenzollerns rather than the Habsburgs, but the clamor for parliamentary government would be stilled by a great national triumph won under monarchical authority. Domestic, national, and international issues of the greatest import were involved in the diplomatic game of the 1860s, which Bismarck played with such consummate skill.

First he induced the Austrians to join him in a brief and successful war against Denmark for the provinces of Schleswig and Holstein. Then he saw to it that no agreement was reached with Vienna regarding the disposition of the spoils of victory. He still had some hope that the Hofburg could be bribed or frightened into agreeing to Prussian predominance in northern Germany. But when the imperial cabinet refused to back down, he decided to risk all in the Seven Weeks' War. Luck was with him. Prussian arms won a swift victory at Sadowa (Königgrätz), which enabled him to form the North German Confederation. Overnight the hated reactionary prime minister became a national demigod. The patriots walked on clouds, the liberals swallowed their scruples, the particularists were intimidated, the Austrians sulked. Only France openly expressed alarm at the establishment on its eastern frontier of a united Germany, which its statesmen had opposed for more than three centuries. But Napoleon III was no match for Bismarck. The Franco-Prussian War led to the overthrow of the Bonaparte dynasty and to the proclamation of the empire of the Hohenzollerns. While the siege guns were booming around cold, starving Paris, the work of German unification was completed on January 18, 1871, at Prussian headquarters in Versailles.

How should this work be assessed? Those who lived in the state Bismarck created usually found little fault with it. It brought them prosperity, respect, strength, and a sense of accomplishment. After its collapse, however, historians began to wonder about the soundness of the foundation on which it had rested. The German Empire lasted forty-seven years. It was followed by the Weimar Republic, which collapsed within fifteen

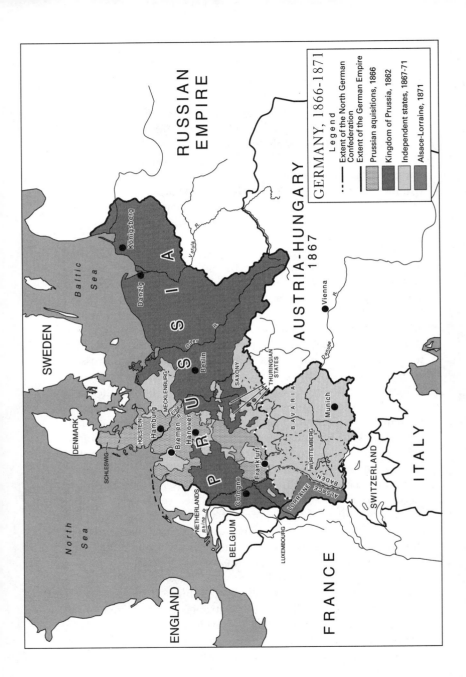

GERMANY, 1866-1871

Legend

--- Extent of the North German Confederation

— Extent of the German Empire

Prussian aquisitions, 1866

Kingdom of Prussia, 1862

Independent states, 1867-71

Alsace-Lorraine, 1871

RUSSIAN EMPIRE

AUSTRIA-HUNGARY 1867

SWEDEN

Baltic Sea

Königsberg

Danzig

Vistula R.

Oder R.

PRUSSIA

Berlin

SAXONY

THURINGIAN STATES

BAVARIA

Munich

Vienna

Danube R.

DENMARK

SCHLESWIG

HOLSTEIN

MECKLENBURG

Hamburg

Bremen

Hanover

WÜRTTEMBERG

BADEN

Frankfurt

ALSACE

LORRAINE

Cologne

Rhine R.

North Sea

NETHERLANDS

BELGIUM

LUXEMBOURG

FRANCE

SWITZERLAND

ITALY

ENGLAND

years. Then came the Third Reich, destroyed twelve years later at the cost of a terrible world conflict. Out of its ruins emerged a diminished and divided people living in the shadow of foreign invasion. Here was a disheartening history of almost a hundred years of disappointed hopes, of wasted efforts, of wars, revolutions, depressions, tyrannies. Could it be that the source of the trouble lay in the way in which a nation was welded out of the diverse lands of Central Europe?

There were those who thought so. To begin with, for some Austrians the verdict of 1866 was hard to accept. They saw in it the tragic end of a historic association of a thousand years between their state and the rest of the Germanic commonwealth, for it left them isolated in a Slavic sea that was eventually bound to overwhelm them. They became the latter-day advocates of the *grossdeutsch* idea, the idea that Germany should be constituted with the participation and under the leadership of Austria. Then there were the French scholars to whom the achievement of a united German state was inextricably bound up with the loss of Alsace and Lorraine. Their dislike of the eternal Boche was probably greatest around the time of World War I. But even after their country regained the lost provinces, they managed to restrain their admiration of Prussian statesmanship. Yet Bismarck was not without his defenders. They contended that in an age of rampant nationalism, the unification of Germany was a historic necessity that could not be realized except through blood and iron. As for the Franco-Prussian War, the jingoes in Paris were as vociferous as those in Berlin. If Napoleon III lost his crown, he had only his own folly to blame.

The fall of the Second French Empire meant a diplomatic revolution in Europe. For the next half-century, Germany was the mightiest state on the Continent, and during the first twenty years of that period, Bismarck was at the helm. His remarkable talents as a statesman were now displayed on a stage greater than that provided by the constitutional conflict in Prussia or even by the long duel with Austria. He had become in effect the arbiter of Europe. How did he use the great power at his disposal? Here is the one point in the lifework of the Iron Chancellor on which there is a high degree of agreement. As a practitioner of the art of diplomacy he is without a peer. His grasp of detail, his insight into motive, his ability to sense the limitations as well as opportunities inherent in each new international development, his tireless search for alternative solutions to every major political problem, his willingness to retreat at the precise moment when risks begin to outweigh advantages: they all bespeak the master craftsman. There can be no gainsaying the technical virtuosity of the man.

Yet virtuosity in a statesman is not without its dangers. The very magnitude of the successes that Bismarck enjoyed tended to make him appear inimitable and to transform his diplomacy into an occult science no one but he could master. William I, a ruler not easily impressed, once exclaimed to his prime minister: "You seem to me at times to be like a rider who juggles on horseback with five balls, never letting one fall." The spell that the wizard of the Wilhelmstrasse cast over his contemporaries was irresistible. What he bequeathed to his country, however, was a legend rather than a vital political creed. Only Bismarck could practice Bismarckian statecraft. Once he fell, his successors found themselves enmeshed in international complications they had never been taught to understand. For he had guarded the secrets of his trade jealously, like some statesman of the age of absolutism, like Mazarin or Kaunitz. But the nineteenth century was a dangerous time for personal diplomacy. The growing complexity of international relations arising out of the advance of technology, the rise of nationalism, and the movement to democracy called for a system of leadership independent of any personality, however brilliant. Because he failed to provide that leadership, the founder of the German Empire must share responsibility for the collapse of his creation.

Many historians, however, have been too concerned with the immediate achievements of Bismarck's diplomacy to speculate about its ultimate implications. Those achievements are admittedly impressive. There is agreement, first of all, that once Germany was united, the Iron Chancellor became a tireless defender of peace in Europe. Not that he was in any sense a pacifist; he was always ready to use armed force to achieve his ends. Had he not deliberately provoked three wars between 1864 and 1870? But he had never accepted the doctrine of boundless expansion; he had never succumbed to the temptation of cheap conquest. The German Empire was for him a "saturated" state, a state that had succeeded in satisfying all of its legitimate territorial aspirations. It had nothing to gain and everything to lose from a major European conflict. That intricate web of alliances and alignments that he spun with such painstaking care had as its objective the maintenance of the status quo. But the achievement of this objective was contingent on the isolation of France, the only major power whose vital national interests could not be satisfied without a war. Some writers have emphasized the pacific aspect of Bismarck's policy, others the anti-French aspect. Actually, the two were opposite sides of a single coin, different but inseparable. They were both essential to the equilibrium that the *Pax Teutonica* maintained in Europe for twenty years.

Bismarck the diplomat has won the admiration of many, the respect of all. Bismarck the prime minister of a constitutional state invites criticism. He was too much the Prussian Junker to understand fully the profound political changes taking place about him during the later years of his life. In democracy he saw only the lust for power of unscrupulous politicians. Socialism was worse still; it meant the alienation of the urban masses from throne and altar, the most cherished institutions of society. As for the Roman Catholic church, it was a foreign establishment propagating unpatriotic doctrines. Its power had to be crushed. The Iron Chancellor threw himself with all his boundless energy into the struggle against those forces that seemed to threaten the values he had spent his life upholding. First there was the *Kulturkampf*, the war against papal influence, which served only to fortify the adherents of the clerical Center party. It was followed by an even more ruthless campaign against socialism, with the same disappointing results. The Social Democratic party was driven underground, but it managed to survive and even increase in strength. Bismarck could still act with daring and imagination. During the 1880s he broke with the prevalent creed of laissez-faire individualism, introducing the first comprehensive system of social legislation in the world. But insurance of the industrial worker against sickness, accident, and old age failed to exorcise the specter of Marxism. In the end the chancellor was forced to contemplate

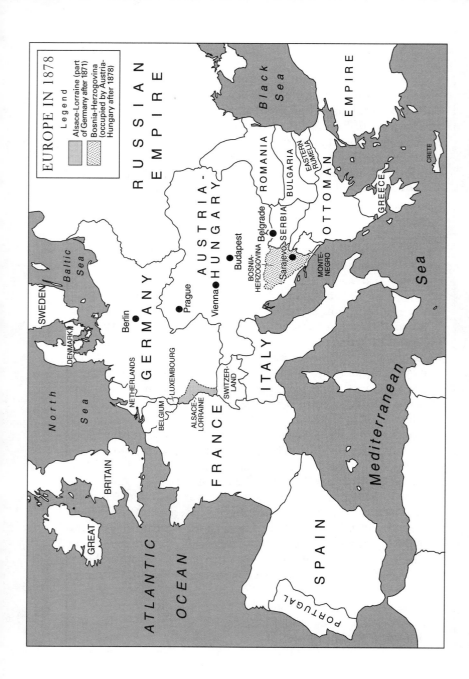

EUROPE IN 1878

Legend

Alsace-Lorraine (part of Germany after 1871)

Bosnia-Herzogovina (occupied by Austria-Hungary after 1878)

RUSSIAN EMPIRE

Black Sea

Baltic Sea

SWEDEN

DENMARK

NETHERLANDS

BELGIUM

LUXEMBOURG

GERMANY

Berlin

Prague

AUSTRIA-HUNGARY

Budapest

Vienna

SWITZER-LAND

ALSACE-LORRAINE

FRANCE

ITALY

BOSNIA-HERZOGOVINA

Sarajevo

Belgrade

SERBIA

MONTE-NEGRO

ROMANIA

BULGARIA

EASTERN RUMELIA

OTTOMAN EMPIRE

GREECE

CRETE

North Sea

GREAT BRITAIN

ATLANTIC OCEAN

SPAIN

PORTUGAL

Mediterranean Sea

a coup d'état leading to a fundamental alteration of the state that he himself had founded.

He never put this plan into effect. The same royal authority that he had defended so brilliantly throughout his career was now used to encompass his downfall. The young William II who came to the throne in 1888 was too impetuous and too ambitious to accept the tutelage of any man. The contest between emperor and chancellor could have only one outcome. The aging giant was unceremoniously forced into retirement, where he continued to grumble his displeasure with the course followed by the new masters of Germany. He lived long enough to see the beginning disintegration of his lifework. But that work was probably doomed in any event. Bismarck had succeeded in discrediting representative institutions and in weakening the party system. He never encouraged independence in those around him, refusing to tolerate anyone whose talents might possibly compete with his own. Especially in his later years he became insufferably domineering, so that his fall was greeted by many of those who knew him best with a deep sigh of relief. He had never recognized that an enduring political system cannot be the achievement of any one man, whatever his strength or determination. He was admittedly no doctrinaire, no phrasemonger. He always stood head and shoulders above the narrow-minded landed aristocrats from whom he had sprung. But with all his intellectual suppleness and perception, he never freed himself completely from the illusion that the old can be preserved indefinitely if it is only made to look like new. History has demonstrated the impossibility of his dream, but through sheer political wizardry he came as close to realizing it as any statesman can approach the impossible.

What is the Bismarckian legacy to our own time? As with everything else about the Iron Chancellor, historians differ. But never has there been as much criticism of his accomplishment as today. The ultimate collapse of everything for which he worked was bound to raise doubts about his methods and objectives. His exaltation of the policy of blood and iron encouraged among his countrymen a worship of power at the expense of justice. His rejection of a federalist solution of the political problems confronting Central Europe led to growing national tension and to an irreconcilable conflict between Slav and Teuton. Austria ceased to play its traditional role as leader and tutor of its neighbors to the east and south. Deprived of its historic mission, it atrophied and disintegrated. Germany too was unable to develop a healthy existence within the framework provided by the Hohenzollern empire. The golden memories of Sadowa and Sedan have long been extinguished by lost world wars, disastrous inflations, territorial losses, population expulsions, concentration camps, and gas chambers. Perhaps the entire work of unification was built on a false foundation. Bismarck's critics also point to his failure to train his nation in the art of self-government. The frailty of democratic institutions in Germany contributed to totalitarianism, to world conflict, and to the devastation of a continent. Europe today is in a sense still paying for the mistakes of the 1860s.

But the Iron Chancellor has his admirers as well. Nor can they be dismissed as mere tub-thumping chauvinists repeating the perennial slogans of professional patriotism. Many of them are scholars of the first rank who see in Bismarck precisely those qualities of moderation and reasonableness that the statesmanship of our own day needs so desperately. At no time did he preach doctrines of racial superiority or unlimited conquest. He always believed in a balance of power resting upon the secure existence of several major states. Germany was to have a primary but not a preponderant position in the councils of Europe. He consistently rejected all claims to totalitarian power on the part of government, and even bureaucratic arbitrariness was a weapon he used sparingly. He liked to play the bluff Junker, strutting in military uniform and indulging in such rodomontade as: "We Germans fear God and nothing else in the world." Actually, he was always careful to respect the vital interests of other nations, unless they conflicted directly with those of his own. Even his treatment of political opponents revealed a restraint that disappointed the extremists in his camp. The Progressives, the Conservatives, the Centrists, the Socialists, the Poles—they all attacked him repeatedly in parliament and press. But he never proposed to deal with them in the time-honored fashion of dictators by putting them up against a wall and ordering the firing squad to shoot. The barbarities of

National Socialism would no doubt have horrified him. Friedrich Meinecke recounts that a Danish friend admitted to him during the Third Reich: "You know I cannot love Bismarck, but now I must say: Bismarck belongs to *our* world."

It is clear that the time for a definitive assessment of the Iron Chancellor has still not arrived. It may never come, for each successive generation seems to find a new meaning in his career. As our experiences change us, so we change our interpretation of the experiences of others. We are always writing history anew. The outcome of World War I forces us to rethink the Franco-Prussian War. The fact that democracy failed in Germany in 1933 suggests a new evaluation of the constitutional conflict in Prussia in 1862–1866. The New Deal calls to mind the social legislation of the 1880s. The existence of the North Atlantic Treaty Organization invites us to study once again the Triple Alliance. The unification of Germany in 1990 reminds us of the unification of Germany in 1871. Yet the inescapable conclusion that historical understanding will be different tomorrow from what it is today, just as today it is different from what it was yesterday, should not lead us to a paralyzing relativism. We have the duty to sit in judgment on the past in the light of our standard of right and wrong. But in order to judge fairly, we must familiarize ourselves with the facts of the case; we must weigh with care the pros and cons. In the case of Bismarck the verdict is particularly difficult. Like the spirit of Caesar, his ghost walks abroad among us, raising questions that are as pertinent to our own time as to his. To answer them, we must examine our own attitudes toward the crucial beliefs and institutions of society. We must ponder the nature of political democracy, national sovereignty, military might, diplomatic hegemony, economic justice. In the search for a solution of the Bismarckian enigma, we will of necessity achieve a deeper understanding of the problems facing us in the critical times in which we live.

Variety of
Opinion

*He was not striving for world-dominion nor for boundless power,
but for the means to secure and strengthen his Prussian Fatherland. So much acquisition of power and of territory as was necessary for this he laid hold of with iron grasp—so much and no
more. The intoxication of victory never disordered his judgment,
nor got the mastery over his fixed principles of moderation.*

Heinrich von Sybel

*.... that extraordinary man, the craftiest of foxes, the boldest of
lions, who had the art of fascinating and of terrifying, of making
of truth itself an instrument of falsehood; to whom gratitude, forgiveness of injuries, and respect for the vanquished were as entirely unknown as all other noble sentiments save that of devotion
to his country's ambition; who deemed legitimate everything that
contributes to success and who, by his contempt for the importunities of morality, dazzled the imagination of mankind.*

Émile Ollivier

*A system which requires a great man in each generation sets itself
an almost insurmountable challenge, if only because a great man
tends to stunt the emergence of strong personalities. When the
novelty of Bismarck's tactics had worn off and the originality of
his conception came to be taken for granted, lesser men strove to
operate his system while lacking his sure touch and almost artistic
sensitivity. As a result, what had been the manipulation of factors*

in a fluid situation eventually led to the petrification of the inter-national system which produced World War I.

Henry A. Kissinger

We may criticize Bismarck for many good reasons, for paving the way to some fatal trends of our days, but while doing so we cannot very well overlook the fundamental fact that Hitler, in almost every respect, did precisely what the founder of the Reich had re-fused to do. Many of those who were under the heel inside or out-side of Germany, had an appreciation of this fact. And thus the word of the Danish historian may be taken up once more as a summary which draws the essential frontier line: Bismarck cer-tainly "belonged to our world," that is, to the anti-Hitlerian world.

Hans Rothfels

In his Thoughts and Recollections *he declares that his aim was to earn the confidence of lesser and greater powers by a peaceful, just, honest and conciliatory policy. It almost sounds like a belated pallia-tion of his essentially Machiavellian statesmanship. Yet the further we carry our researches, the clearer is the evidence that he was only putting into words the fundamental principle of his actions.*

Erich Brandenburg

One must regard Bismarck as a borderline case. He still had in mind to some extent the conception of a synthesis of power and culture as it was understood by the leaders of the movement for German unity. These leaders themselves, with Treitschke at their head, originally were seriously offended by Bismarck's first steps in the period of the constitutional conflict, but became his defenders and admirers as a consequence of the war of 1866. The result was that in the synthesis of power and culture, of the things of the state and the things of the spirit, the preponderance slowly but steadily shifted further over to the side of power and its domain.

Friedrich Meinecke

His had been a great career, beginning with three wars in eight years and ending with a period of twenty years during which he worked for the peace of Europe, despite countless opportunities to embark on further enterprises with more than an even chance of success. No other statesman of his standing had ever before shown the same great moderation and sound political sense of the possible and the desirable.

William L. Langer

He made shift with the old means and the old purposes. This had never before led to enduring order; now the passions were all aroused as well. Bismarck took part in this release from control. He believed that he could utilize the new impulsion to be found in the crowd for the power of his state, and at the same time limit it by a rational system called reason of state. He did not come to a realization that in a world of such confusions there are tasks which go far beyond the state, and that it was becoming extremely necessary to bring the state back to its original purpose, to help establish the good, the right, the higher order. His position remained that the statesman's task consisted in nothing more than development of the state.

Franz Schnabel

Bismarck as a young man. This drawing shows Bismarck in the early 1830s, at the age of seventeen or eighteen, while a student at the University of Göttingen. He is portrayed as a handsome, dandyish young man more interested in dueling and drinking beer than in writing term papers or cramming for exams. (Archiv für Kunst und Geschichte, Berlin)

PART

I

The Making of a Statesman

Erich Marcks

A Country Squire

A decade after Bismarck's death, the eminent German scholar Erich Marcks published the first volume of what promised to become the classic life of the Iron Chancellor, but at the time of Marcks's death in 1938, the next part of the biography had still not appeared. Perhaps the task was too great for even his considerable talents. What we have is only a fragment, a fragment suggesting the heroic proportions of the unfinished design. In its grand scope and meticulous detail, it reveals the admiration of the biographer for his subject. Marcks emphasizes in the following selection the importance of Bismarck's experiences as a landed aristocrat.

Source: Erich Marcks, *Bismarck: Eine Biographie, 1815–1851,* 1951, pp. 150–155, published by Deutsche Verlags-Anstalt GmbH, translated by Theodore S. Hamerow and William W. Beyer.

During those years he [Bismarck] was a farmer pure and simple. He was active on various commissions of the Regenwald Agricultural Association in 1842, 1844, and 1845, was once recommended by it for a royal prize, borrowed from it (1843) many books and periodicals on agriculture and economics. A neighbor of Bismarck later told von Keudell about his study of topography in maps and books, and about his amazing knowledge of the soil and value of estates in Pomerania, the Mark, and the Magdeburg region. But above all, letters to various members of his family reflect again and again his physical and spiritual dedication to farming. They tell about his activities, about the weather, about crop conditions, about horses and laborers, about frosts, diseases, natural calamities and prices, about his own estate and the situation of others, and about his observations on economic conditions abroad. A part of his account books has been preserved. There are long sections in his own handwriting, the entries arranged by date, neatly and carefully classified under various categories of receipts and expenditures, balanced for each month, the vertical letters pressed close together. Among the receipts those from wool are most important, but on one occasion there is also mention of a small sum won in gambling. The expenditures column includes large amounts and small, business outlays and personal expenses: machinery, seed, wages, insurance, taxes and county fees, and then the costs of travel, innkeeper's bills, gratuities, modest gambling debts, but also an entry "50 taler for the victims of the fire in Trieglaff" (1845). Bismarck borrowed money and paid it back to businessmen, friends, and relatives, and in turn helped the latter out. His published letters have told us much about his business affairs; for example, about his unexpected trouble with taxes during his trip to France in 1842, when his father and brother proved very helpful. These financial difficulties never ceased entirely, not even at Schönhausen. Yet there can be no doubt that his work was highly profitable. He wrote in 1884 to one of his friends from the university days at Göttingen, affecting the bantering tone of a student: "For five years I have lived alone in the country and devoted myself with some success to the enlargement of my school allowance." The figures with which he explained to his fiancée (February 13, 1847) the increase in value of his three estates speak for themselves: what he had vainly tried to sell for 150,000 taler in 1838 was now valued at 200,000, and even that estimate was too low.

Did this work also give him the freedom and the joy of creativity which he had expected when he wrote to Countess Bismarck-Bohlen at the time of his change of occupation? "I have recovered through experience from illusions about the rustic happiness of an inveterate farmer, with double-entry bookkeeping and the study of chemistry," he told his fiancée nine years later. But in the meantime he had devoted himself to his work and been profoundly influenced by it. In spite of his growing complaints, he was a dedicated farmer and in a sense remained one all his life. It is not only the letters to his family reporting his adjustment to living in Schönhausen which prove this point. Even from Versailles he kept watch over the estate at Varzin with surprising solicitude, composing long written instructions as if there were no war to wage and no German Empire to build.

He came to identify himself with his environment as never before. He worked in the garden with great fondness. How difficult was it for him in 1847 to part from his "plants and lawns, from the white bridges and benches." He had planned to build a new house. He regarded Kniephof with all of the nobleman's love for land, a love which he then transferred to Schönhausen; he regarded it with all the tenderness of his childhood memories. He himself had felt during those years the patriarchal affection which he later praised in his article of 1848. His relationship to the laborers who had dutifully served his father for so long was full of mutual trust. In a letter to his fiancée he describes their tearful farewells and their fears that the future manager of the estate might prove unkind. But he was not the only witness on this point. In 1899 Reinhold von Thadden, the son of Bismarck's neighbors in Trieglaff, wrote his recollections of the great man, recollections which tell us much about those youthful years. He too remembered how Bismarck admired the cheerful friendliness of Senfft-Pilsach toward his workers, and how his own dealings with those beneath him were exemplary, completely free of any haughtiness. According to his friend Moritz von Blanckenburg, Bismarck spoke to each of his servants as if to a member of his own circle of acquaintances. In January 1844 Blanckenburg himself wrote to him in the course of a chatty, friendly letter:

> *Otto, are you not a kind person . . . are you not a master with a warm heart for your servants, a master who is just to all and gives each his*

due . . . ? We both have the same calling on earth, and I would be very pleased, if I could get along with the people who work for me as well as is commonly said about you.

Only in those years apparently did he become entirely fluent in Low German. And only then did he get to know the country and its people, by dealing with them directly. Years later at the dinner table he enjoyed describing Pomeranian types, Jews, noblemen. He relied on his sympathy and familiarity with the peasants, with their way of thinking and feeling, with their needs and problems, in many of the great speeches which he delivered as chancellor in support of his tax and tariff policies. The von Thaddens learned in 1844 with pleasant surprise how well he could deal with rustics, when he represented them after a destructive fire in negotiations with the peasants of Trieglaff. And only in those years did he acquire that vast knowledge of the soil and of all things pertaining to it with which he was still able to astonish city people in his eighties. Here was a land of wide horizons, resembling the region where his ancestors had lived. . . . It was a land which rewarded only patient effort, a land which tended to encourage sobriety. He learned to observe it in detail in the life of the smallest creature in his park, as well as on a large scale on his rolling fields and meadows. He directed his supervising glance at daily growth and development. Like every countryman he came to feel the great human dependence on the powers of nature, on weather, on rain, on frost, on pestilence. As owner of his land he no doubt experienced what the greatest rustic poet of our people has praised as the unobtrusive yet urgent lesson of agriculture: the repose which devoutly anticipates the germination and development of the bud, the moderation which must admit every day that trees do not grow as high as the sky, the assurance that crops can be harvested only "when the color and the weight of the fruit tell that the time has come." He also learned to be observant, matter-of-fact, realistic; a limited occupation taught him to master a well-defined field of endeavor and its problems. He had become a huntsman early in life, and now he pursued the sport more than ever. The hunt trained him to scout, to reconnoiter, to lie in wait, to watch, and then act quickly and effectively. He rode far and wide on his loyal Caleb through the Pomeranian countryside, "over many a mile, happy and sad, angry and calm, past moors and fields, past lakes and houses and people." Even as an old man he enjoyed rides and trips, gazing about him and trying to see all. A quarter of a century later he could still surprise Reinhold Thadden with the infallible accuracy of his recollections about the boundaries of parishes and the points of the compass.

The impressions of those long years in the country greatly affected the policies and decisions of his later life. It has long been noted that in the extraordinary richness of his language the most characteristic, novel, and perceptive expressions are always derived from the country, from houses and roofs and barrels and pots, from riding and travel, from streets and bridges, from farming with all its skills and sorrows, from horse trading, from the hunt. Soil, animals and plants, weather and heat and disease provided him with insight and comparison. The proverbial, the popular, the natural grew on him, rose to his lips. Even bills of exchange and mortgages were familiar to him and became part of his vocabulary. Everything was experienced reality. "By the time of the next partridge hunt I'll be married," he announces laconically to his brother in April 1847.

All this was not new in his character. His language had from the beginning suggested rural, aristocratic primitiveness and tradition. He knew as early as 1838 what drew him so passionately to the country. But the full realization must have come later; only later was his life filled with it. Above all, only later did he become master of his estate, and that was what he had always desired most of all. He could now command his land and his people; he no longer needed to obey. As lord of the manor he kept the record in his large, firm script whenever the mayor, the preacher, or the schoolmaster from Jarchelin squabbled about fees. He exercised police power. Although a free member of the governing class, he soon subordinated himself more and more to the aristocratic government of the country. Still, he had to make his decisions independently, and he led a lonely life on his estate, like many of his class. Yet he was separated from the others by a wide gulf. Even this loneliness of which he was to complain so often with the passage of time belongs to the formative forces of this period of his life, and is related to his freedom and pride. The oak grows broadest and strongest when it grows alone. He knew that very well. On November 3, 1870, he spoke at

Versailles about the difference between the city and the country. Because of its direct contact with nature, the countryside makes people more practical. The big city makes them too clever. It creates mass opinions out of thin air, out of rumors and counterrumors, without any basis in fact. It breeds unshakable mass superstitions, which spin a web around people and soon appear to them duties and obligations: "Where so many men live close together, individual characteristics disappear easily, they melt together." It does not matter whether in these chatty observations Count Bismarck was being fair to the individualism which the city and its culture develop, the modern, democratic individualism of whose unattractive side he spoke. The point is that he revealed a deep-seated feeling which he had acquired in the country. He believed in a differently conceived, unrefined, autocratic individualism; he believed in an aristocratic personality rooted in the soil, completely self-reliant, acting freely and generously, a personality growing out of the past and growing into every new epoch, nourished by ancient tradition, and yet an expression of eternally youthful individualistic forces. This is the personality which ripened in him during his years in Pomerania, which intermingled with the great fullness of his most intimate qualities. This is the personality which strengthened and broadened and grew to those heights to which it was one day triumphantly to exalt a people.

Hajo Holborn

Formative Intellectual Experiences

Hajo Holborn belonged to the generation of German scholars that reached maturity under the Weimar Republic. While still only in his thirties, he won a reputation as a leading scholar in the field of modern

Source: Hajo Holborn, "Bismarck's Realpolitik," From *Journal of the History of Ideas*, 1960, pp. 84–91. Reprinted with permission from the Journal of the History of Ideas, Inc.

history. With the coming of the Third Reich he emigrated to the United States, where he became professor at Yale University. He dealt in his writings with the Renaissance and Reformation, with diplomatic history and the philosophy of history, as well as with Germany. His treatment of Bismarck is not unappreciative, but it avoids the uncritical adulation of so many of the Iron Chancellor's biographers. Here he examines the ideas and ideals that shaped the mind of the statesman.

In a famous letter to Leopold von Gerlach Bismarck expressed his belief that "nobody ever loses the stamp which the age of youthful impressions has imposed on him," and he distanced himself from the older man who had formed his ideals during the war of liberation from Napoleon. Friedrich Meinecke already has called attention to the relatively cool attitude which Bismarck always displayed with regard to the period of Prussian reform and liberation. To be sure, the struggle against foreign domination seemed to him a worthy cause, but he denied that the simultaneous attempt of the Prussian reformers to establish an ideal German state had made an essential contribution to eventual liberation. The philosophical idealism of the age of Kant, Fichte, and Schleiermacher, in which a Stein, Humboldt, Scharnhorst, Gneisenau, and Boyen had found the expression of their own ideal longings, was alien to Bismarck.

Bismarck grew up when the German philosophy of the classic age ceased to satisfy the hearts of the young. In the years after 1815, the German philosophy had grown more scholastic, and the deep human experiences which had once led to its creation were largely hidden under a crust of abstract logical thought. The generation which began to take the stage after 1835, the year in which David Friedrich Strauss published his *Life of Jesus,* criticized idealism for its failure to understand the new reality and to give a positive direction to life. Strauss, and those after him, Ludwig Feuerbach, Bruno Bauer, and Karl Marx, all manifested the gathering trend toward realism, which with these Young Hegelians, however, assumed at first an even more intensely rationalistic tinge than with the old Hegel.

It was this rationalism that Bismarck resented. As a youth he had received religious instruction from Schleiermacher, the warmhearted philosopher and patriotic preacher whose vindication of religion and emphasis on sentiment and feeling had meant to an earlier generation the release from the exclusive rule of reason. Bismarck discovered in Schleiermacher's teachings only an intellectualistic pantheism, which he proceeded to combine with a skepticism that denied the possibility of any human knowledge of God's plan of the world and of the place of the individual in it. This agnosticism, which according to Bismarck derived chiefly from Spinoza and the Stoics, always welled up as one important element in Bismarck's thinking, and particularly in his late years.

Bismarck's search for the concrete beauty of life never fully relieved the boredom and melancholy that his skepticism produced. He was always close to nature. His wide readings in German classic literature and most of all in Shakespeare, as well as the music of Beethoven, gave his imaginative mind models of heroic men and great tragic situations. Shakespeare had been declared the poetic genius by Herder and the young Goethe. Bismarck fully accepted the modern German outlook that originated with the literary revolution of *Sturm und Drang*. He desired passion and sentiment and, therefore, found much of the work of the romantic writers to his liking. Yet it was not the romanticism which looked for an escape from the realities into a realm of artificial beauty or of religion that attracted him, but those romantic efforts that led to a clearer grasp of reality. Through its devotion to the unique value of individuality, romanticism, indeed, prepared the ground for a more realistic study of the world, as the growth of modern historical studies in Germany showed. With sharp and piercing eyes the young Bismarck looked around in his own personal world and early revealed an extraordinary gift for literary narration and characterization.

In the school of romanticism the cult of personality flourished to excess, and in this respect also Bismarck was a true child of his age. For some time Byron was dearer to him than Shakespeare. The young Bismarck gave free rein to his pugnaciousness in dozens of duels, and he plunged headlong into stormy love affairs. Eventually he refused to enter, as a Prussian of his class was expected to do, the government services or make the army his career. "I do not like superiors," he exclaimed, and another time, "I want to make music as I like it or not at all." Thus he withdrew to the family estates, which he managed very effectively. But only part of his energies were engaged. There was time left to resume the search for the meaning of life, and even more to parade his self-confidence before the neighbors by audacious acts of sportsmanship or by extravagant pranks. The unbridled cult of individuality was threatening to corrode any serious purpose of his existence. It was his conversion to a positive theistic Christian view and his marriage, in 1847, that ended this period of life of the "mad Junker," as he had been called.

Bismarck's religious conversion has been much studied. Practically no one has questioned the sincerity of his religious feelings, though many have pointed out that Bismarck's adoption of a theistic faith was closely related to his wish to be accepted by his devout future bride and her Pietistic family. The sudden death of a close friend, Marie von Blanckenburg, and the love for her friend Johanna von Puttkamer naturally gave his questions about life a new urgency, and the religion of his friends made a serious impression on him. Still, there was a strong voluntaristic side to Bismarck's decision. By embracing a personal God he set an end to his drifting in doubts. At the same time his marriage gave him a firm anchorage in Prussian society, in which he had his natural roots, but from which so far he had longed to flee into a world of free and heroic action. Together with his pantheism he dismissed what he occasionally called his republicanism. In the same breath he won a wife and a religious and political faith. He had chosen his fundamental position when a little later the revolution drew him into the political arena, first as a parliamentarian, subsequently as a diplomat, and finally as a minister of state.

Yet before appraising his statecraft we must stress that Bismarck did not become a Pietist in 1847. He placed his trust in a personal God, whom he accepted as the creator and king of the universe, but he obviously cared little for Christian dogmas. He prayed to God, whose ways he considered unfathomable and whom he did not think to move by his prayer. But he said — probably unaware that the words could be found in Schleiermacher's *Glaubenslehre* — that the usefulness of prayer lay in submission to a strong power. His new belief in a personal God was actually still compatible with much of Bismarck's original skepticism. Though less general, it was almost as subjective as his earlier notions. As a matter of fact, in his later years he seems to have moved even closer to his early ideas.

It was probably impossible in nineteenth century German Protestantism to find any conception of the Christian Church as a divinely ordained community which possessed a moral authority independent of the state. The Protestant churches were essentially state-controlled institutes for preaching. The Pietists were critics of this state-system and often opposed to ministers. But all they could do was to form small conventicles such as those in which Bismarck had come in contact with Pietistic orthodoxy. Bismarck never cultivated any group worship after his conversion and favored the state-church, though he himself, as he put it, did not wish to be "edified by mouth of ministers." Yet since he suspected ministers of being desirous of power, he preferred having them under the supervision of the state. Another observation can be made. The new faith helped to give Bismarck's whole thinking a firm orientation. It also made him act not only with greater determination but also with a heightened sense of moral responsibility. Yet it did not change his relations with his fellow-men. He remained the cavalier, normally polite to his equals, well-mannered and benevolent even to members of the lesser classes, but on the other hand reckless in forcing people to serve him or humiliating them if they refused, or were suspected of refusing, cooperation. The man who lay awake whole nights "hating," who could perhaps forget but not forgive — all this according to his own testimony — had not through his conversion become a new man.

Friedrich Meinecke has suggested that the decline of German idealism in the 1830s might be responsible for Bismarck's turning away from idealism to orthodoxy and thereby from liberalism to conservatism. He thought that if Bismarck had found a philosophy which would have answered the burning questions of his personal growth, he might have become a more liberal statesman like Cavour. Although I agree with Meinecke that the formation of Bismarck's personal convictions cannot be explained outside of his age, the question raised by Meinecke defies a solution because it is impossible to visualize different historical circumstances while assuming that the person involved would remain the same. Bismarck actually absorbed certain influences of German idealism, and the subjective and voluntaristic religion which he adopted was clearly "post-idealistic," but the liberal and humanitarian elements of the classic German philosophy found no response in him.

In 1838 the young Gladstone wrote his first book in which he pleaded for the closest relation between church and state. Without a sanctifying principle, he argued, the state would become a mere machine with no other function than that of registering and executing opinions of the popular will like the hands of a clock. Gladstone was then still an ardent Tory, and his theses were warmly applauded by Frederick William IV of Prussia and his conservative friends. It is well known how greatly Gladstone's political views changed in his later years, when he became a liberal out of Christian convictions. But as little as he gave up his Christian belief did he deviate from his early demand that creative politics called for "sanctifying principles." Bismarck saw in Gladstone more than in any other statesman on the contemporary European scene his ideological opposite. He was wrong, however, in asserting that Gladstone — or, as he labelled him with one of his strongest vituperative expressions, "*Professor*" Gladstone — was ruining England, nor could he know that a Gladstonean Professor Wilson was destined to become the foremost destroyer of the German monarchy.

What made Bismarck a fiery enemy of Gladstone was both the liberalism and insistence of Gladstone on a Christian program in politics. Bismarck soon parted company with his early conservative associates, the members of the so-called Christian-Germanic circle, with regard to the application of Christian principles to practical politics. In Bismarck's view, the world and its orders were created by God and the course of history directed by him. The existing political institutions, consequently, were not made by men nor could they be altered by ideal constructions of human reason, as the liberals proposed. But the concrete plan of God was unknown to man, except that it was clear that in all history the decisions had been reached by power used for selfish interests, and that this *raison d'état* could be studied and acted upon. This nature of the political life of the world was to him divinely instituted and, therefore, essentially immutable, although life was a continuous conflict and struggle. To hope that men could change the nature of politics would be sinfully arrogant and would mean to meddle in divine government.

The statesman might gain, however, at rare moments a fleeting adumbration of divine action on a higher plane.

These ideas excluded the possibility of Christianizing the state and the international life. There was no ideal state, let alone an ideal international order, but only the concrete order of history which demanded from everybody obedience to the positive law. This Bismarckian attitude has been called Lutheran by historical students of Bismarck, and it is quite true that his political conceptions showed the earmarks of the political thinking that had developed in German Lutheranism. But it would be erroneous to assume that Bismarck's and Luther's opinions were identical. The world of states was for Luther not the arena for the realization of the kingdom of God. Luther admitted that statecraft required special political knowledge though to him this was not identical with the *raison d'état*. And while Luther did not believe that the state as such was a Christian institution, he considered it the duty of every individual Christian to assert within the public life a special moral attitude derived from his Christian faith. In this respect Bismarck's early conservative companions, particularly Friedrich Julius Stahl, were closer to Luther than Bismarck.

But Bismarck did not deny that at least the statesman himself, if he was a Christian, was bound by certain specific principles. The exercise of power was not to aim at personal ends but was a calling to preserve the natural order of things and to serve the state. No doubt, these were important moral restraints which reflected genuine ideas of Luther, though in somewhat weaker fashion. Luther justified war only in self-defense and recommended that Christian princes should rather suffer some occasional injustice and forget about their own "reputation" than go to a war that would bring calamitous suffering to their people. Bismarck repeatedly condemned preventive wars and never accepted war lightheartedly, but he did accept it as a means for accomplishing his political aims. Also, he ruled out wars for prestige, but not for the honor of the state.

The outlook on life and history with which Bismarck entered politics endowed the prevailing political conditions of Prussia with an aura of sanctity. Not only the monarchy but also the traditional class society of Prussia, with the Junker estate as the dominant social group, was in his eyes the God-willed order of things, and its maintenance by all means of political cunning the unquestionable duty of the statesman. Liberalism, which for him comprised every movement derived from the ideas of the American and French revolutions, was the sworn enemy of a healthy political life, since it attempted to replace historically developed forms of life by an arbitrary system of man-made institutions. In Bismarck's thought any kind of liberalism was bound to lead to government by parties, and this weakening of the authority of the state would bring forth the chaos of a social republic, from which a people could be freed only by a regime of fire and sword. On the other hand, a regime of naked force was disliked by Bismarck, although many governmental measures which he recommended or adopted were of highly doubtful legality. He was not even a champion of an unrestricted absolute monarchy. He objected to the suppression of the independent rights of the nobility by rulers. Moreover, absolutism fed that "boa constrictor," bureaucracy, which was tyrannical but at the same time a breeding ground of liberal notions.

These Bismarckian conceptions might have made this Junker a radical reactionary after the breakdown of the German revolution, radical to the extent of demanding the suppression of those moderate German-national and liberal trends that had existed in Prussia before 1848, and even more of the concessions made during the revolution, of which the Prussian constitution of 1850 was the most important grant. But in spite of his brazenly contemptuous attitude towards democracy and liberalism during the revolution, Bismarck was not found among the extreme die-hards in the 1850s. A parliament, in particular, seemed to offer many potential advantages. Through it the conservatives could assert their views — if need be even against crown and bureaucracy — and Bismarck never forgot that the king had faltered in the early months of the revolution. But the chief value of a parliament was the chance it provided for entering on a contest with the liberal forces. Bismarck realized that these forces could not be conquered by mere repression and that the ideological errors and the political futility of modern democracy would have to be shown up by word and deed.

While Bismarck, therefore, accepted a parliament, he remained a deadly foe of parliamentary government. The monarchical government was always to retain a basis of power of its own and for this reason never surrender its exclusive control of the army and foreign affairs. During the revolution of 1848–1849 Bismarck had seen that the Austrian and Prussian monarchies recovered their strength because their armies remained loyal to the dynastic cause. He had also observed the weaknesses in German liberalism, how the fear of social revolution had impaired its aggressive spirit, how the political moderates and radicals had divided, and how the ideas about the forms of the desired national union, *grossdeutsch vs. kleindeutsch*, had produced further splits in German liberalism. He had also noticed that the social and economic program of the liberals failed to keep its early large following united, and that individual groups could be bought rather cheaply by the old governments. It had not escaped his attention that the majority of the German people, especially the peasant and working classes, were still politically quiescent and that it might be feasible to mobilize them for the support of monarchical government, as Louis Bonaparte had done.

Lothar Gall

The Road to Damascus

The best biography of Bismarck to appear in Germany after World War II, the most balanced, the most judicious, was written by Lothar Gall. Too young to have been directly involved in the bitter ideological conflicts of the Third Reich, the author managed to steer a middle course between the nationalistic admirers of the Iron Chancellor and his inveterate critics who see him only as the forerunner of Hitler. The book's protagonist appears here as a "white revolutionary" who transformed the system of government of his country in order to preserve its traditional political relationships and conservative social values. Gall presents a perceptive account of Bismarck's years in Frankfurt as the Prussian representative at the Diet of the German Confederation, the period when the Junker of Schönhausen became a convert to the cause of national unification under the Hohenzollerns.

Source: Lothar Gall, *Bismarck: The White Revolutionary*, 1986, Vol. I, pp. 98–102, Unwin Hyman Ltd.

In Frankfurt . . . his [Bismarck's] life-style further reinforced the impression of a proudly self-assured outsider who boasted of nothing but his country's power and his own special relationships with his monarch and with his head of government. The opinions of many of his Frankfurt colleagues chimed with this impression. As the Austrian envoy Count Thun put it with polite restraint soon after Bismarck's arrival, the new Prussian envoy appeared to him "to belong exclusively to that party that has an eye only to the specific interests of Prussia and places no great faith in what can be achieved by the Federal Diet. Having never previously been in the diplomatic service or even held public office, he has no proper knowledge of affairs and argues all matters purely in accordance with his previous parliamentary experience." The emotions and antipathies that his behaviour was capable of arousing among his diplomatic colleagues are reflected in the vehemence — unusual even in secret diplomatic communications — with which Thun's successor, Baron Prokesch von Osten, characterized him: "Behind his occasional gentlemanliness, an arrogant, mean disposition full of swollen-headed self-conceit; with no awareness of law, lazy, lacking in sound knowledge and in respect for the same; a skilful sophist and word-twister full of petty and underhand resources; full of envy and hatred of Austria, hence also his continuous campaign against the presidential powers; a non-believer, but one who carries his Protestantism like a banner." And even Count Rechberg, the future Austrian Foreign Minister, spoke in 1855 of how "with his petty politics and with his choice of means, in which he allows no considerations to deter him, not even those that a gentleman owes to his government as he does to himself," Bismarck had "seriously harmed his reputation with his colleagues."

Certainly none of these verdicts — and they were backed up by a host of others — does justice either to Bismarck himself or to the kind of calculation, political perspicacity and sheer political passion, overriding all other considerations, that governed his conduct in Frankfurt. But they do serve to characterize the atmosphere in which he moved, and which he himself spread about him, and with it the background that undoubtedly influenced his behaviour and his political ideas and attitudes to a greater degree than a purely abstract exposé of the positions and problems is often prepared to concede.

This is particularly true of his relationship to Austria, now rein-
stated as the leading power in the German Confederation. People
have often spoken in this connection of a wavering between con-
frontation and co-operation, of what for all its antagonisms was in
many ways an ambivalent relationship. However, the immediate impression of his life and work in Frankfurt clearly contradicts this. A
great deal of evidence of such wavering can certainly be adduced,
evidence that was provided by Bismarck himself over a period of
many years and that moreover tallies completely with his basic tactical concept of always, if possible, keeping two paths open. And undoubtedly Rechberg showed great perception when in his verdict
on Bismarck delivered in 1855 he went on: "Ambitious above all
things, he has already shown on several occasions that he knows
how to adapt his opinions to the circumstances. However ardent his
hatred of Austria may appear today, in altered circumstances he
would surely not withhold his services from a policy based on reach-
ing an understanding with Austria." But during his Frankfurt period
it was his "hatred of Austria" that clearly predominated — and did
so, moreover, with very much the sort of emotional groundswell
that one senses through Rechberg's words.

Bismarck was convinced that from the point of view of Prussia's
interest as a nation and as a great power the existing situation in
central Europe was intolerable "if only because of our geographical
deformity," that Prussia and Austria were here "breathing each
other's breath" and that in the long run one of them must "yield to
or be forced to yield by the other," and he reiterated that conviction
too often in these years for there to be any possible doubt that it was
sincerely held. In fact at times he became literally entangled in it in
a way that threatened to cloud his sense of reality with illusions of
possibilities for which all domestic, foreign policy and military requirements were lacking. An example was when in the spring of
1859 he remarked in a letter — afterwards quoted repeatedly and
often quite uncritically — to General von Alvensleben about the
war then looming between the Habsburg monarchy and Sardinia-
Piedmont with its French ally, the war of Italian unification: "The
current situation yet again holds the jackpot for us if we just let
Austria's war with France really bite and then move south with all
our armies, carrying the border posts with us in our knapsacks and

banging them in again either at the Lake of Constance or wherever the Protestant confession ceases to predominate." Or when he wrote to Moritz von Blanckenburg on 12 February 1860: "This clinging to the half-Slav, half-Romance hybrid state on the Danube, this whoring with Pope and Emperor is at least as traitorous to Prussia and the evangelical confession, indeed to Germany, as the meanest, most barren Confederation of the Rhine. The most we can lose to France is provinces, and that only for a time, but to Austria we can lose all of Prussia, now and for ever. *Less* than that Vienna is not interested in as an ultimate objective." Ludwig von Gerlach was not entirely wrong when he observed on one occasion: "He does have a tendency to forget the world and its governance for his own notion of it."

But Bismarck made these statements at a time when a change of course in Prussian domestic policy seemed to him to have cut off all hope of his ever acquiring a substantial say in the shaping of his country's foreign policy. This meant that the counterpoise effect of direct responsibility in one form or another was removed in those years. In the years before, however, that counterpoise had been continuously and obviously present, particularly since from the outset Bismarck regarded his envoyship as the first rung on a ladder leading to the top job in the Prussian Foreign Office; he was always as it were anticipating higher responsibilities. This is clear from his exhaustive memoranda even on matters of only peripheral formal concern to the Prussian legation in Frankfurt. As a result, this concentration on Prussia's relations with Austria into which his whole environment, right down to the minor details of social life, continually prodded him did not in the end, despite his occasional obsessions, have a narrowing effect but on the contrary revealed to him for the first time the full dimensions of his own future policy.

For one thing the constant search for constellations within which Prussia could successfully hold its ground against Austria led him finally to reject the whole idea of prior commitments, the whole concept of permanent blocs of individual states, irrespective of whether these were formed on ideological, historical, or any other grounds. And for another — and this was perhaps even more important — he added in this connection, if at first often in the purely theoretical form of diplomatic sand-table exercises, to the traditional instruments of foreign policy, including as possibilities forces and tactics that had scarcely seemed usable as such hitherto. In these two things lay the true significance of the Frankfurt years, which in terms of tangible results yielded virtually nothing. Bismarck was not unjustified in complaining repeatedly of the pointlessness of his work at the "Danaids' water butt in the Eschenheimer Gasse." The years between 1851 and early 1859, the period Bismarck spent in Frankfurt, saw as little change in the constitution of the Confederation, the formal distribution of political weight within it and the functions it performed as it saw — at least up until 1858 — in the overall political situation in central Europe.

This was the period of victorious reaction. Movement and change came either from outside or — with mounting dramatic impact — from the social transformation that, together with its economic preconditions, increasingly constituted a sort of self-generating and unstoppable process. Anyone who for his part was looking for changes of a power-political nature that would benefit his country but had no wish to interfere with the recently reestablished internal balance of power needed to turn his attention to these two spheres. This is just what Bismarck did. And the two spheres, the social and the economic, shaped and determined his politics both as to form and as to content.

A natural consequence of his position was that he was particularly concerned with whatever affected central Europe from outside in a challenging and upsetting manner. But the insights of his student days, his basic understanding of the crucial impulses governing political and social life and the orientation of his public career as originally conceived led him entirely as a matter of course to see foreign relations and foreign policy developments not in isolation but in terms of their interaction with the march of economic and social change and with the shifts in the distribution of political weight and changing constellations of interests that resulted. So it is idle to argue about which sphere, domestic affairs or foreign affairs, enjoyed priority as far as he was concerned and essentially governed his behaviour. His experience was such that both came more and more to form a single unity. Although professionally and by his own inclination his interest centered over long periods on foreign policy, he always saw it as part of so dense a web that the problem of which came first as far as he was concerned simply disappears in practice. If he did occasionally talk about foreign affairs as being for him "an end in themselves" and as counting for "more than the rest," it was only in defending himself against the charge that foreign policy served him as a mere means to an end, in other words that domestic policy took clear precedence over it in his eyes. He never, so far as we know, claimed that the opposite was the case. Indeed we can even say that his predilection for foreign affairs, leaving aside the circumstances of his path through life for the moment, rested not least on his realization that in this sphere the individual, for all his calculations and painstaking analyses, was to a very much greater extent than in other spheres of politics placed in the position of the gambler, whose winning or losing was in the last analysis decided by unpredictable forces.

When after 1871 the questions of the internal constitution and the structuring of relationships within the newly founded Reich came to dominate the scene, he was once again, as he had been as a young man, "bored to death." For him this was "poor hare-hunting," as he exclaimed to a group of parliamentary associates in 1874. "Ah, if it was a question of bagging a big, powerful boar — an Erymanthian boar, why not? — then I'd be with you, then I'd stir my stumps again." His whole life long it was not the implementation of a plan or the application of an idea that attracted him but the challenge and the opportunities associated with a particular situation or a particular pattern of relationships that he came up against, the risk involved in taking up such a challenge. The foregone conclusion interested him as little as the apparent non-starter, even though the former might represent the historically potent and the latter the genuine challenge. The undecided aspects of reality constituted his field. Whether in the context of the historical process they represented problems of peripheral or central importance were in his eyes abstract, philosophical questions that did not concern him or inhibit him in the slightest.

But where were such undecided aspects of reality to be found in greater number than in the sphere of foreign policy, especially in a period when the always highly unstable balance of power in Europe was continually shifting not only for political but above all for economic reasons? If for him foreign affairs counted for "more than the rest" it was for this reason: he ultimately had his roots in personality and not in the thing itself. He thus of course brought to this a "subterranean" element, a deeply subjective and emotional content that, when it found adherents and was even backed up by an ideology, inevitably became destructive in its effects. That is another story, part of the long story of Bismarck's indirect responsibilities, a story that through the medium of blind imitation and success-worship brings out very clearly the darker side of his being.

So there were incentives from many sides for Bismarck to throw himself into his new job with unusual energy and passion and himself become an engine of disturbance and change from the very beginning. This he did by seizing every available opportunity to prod power relationships within the Confederation into movement and in particular to make repeated attacks, both covert and open, on the precedence and effective hegemony of the Habsburg monarchy, claiming that these were merely dictated by the situation and questioning their permanence.

A. J. P. Taylor

A Freudian Approach

Interest in the Iron Chancellor is not confined to German historians. The well-known English scholar A. J. P. Taylor wrote a highly critical biography, portraying his protagonist as a gifted neurotic driven by a need to satisfy his colossal ego. Here is a Bismarck who cannot be interpreted simply as a Prussian Junker, or a Pietistic Lutheran, or even a bold diplomat crossing swords with mighty Austria. His brilliant but unstable personality must be described in the language of psychoanalysis. Taylor wrote with such urbanity and assurance that, like St. Paul, he almost persuades us.

Source: From *Bismarck: The Man and the Statesman* by A. J. P. Taylor. Copyright © 1955 by A. J. P. Taylor. Reprinted by permission of Alfred A. Knopf, Inc.

His father Ferdinand was a typical Junker, sprung from a family as old as the Hohenzollerns — "a Swabian family no better than mine" Bismarck once remarked. Schönhausen itself symbolized their humiliation; for they had received it as compensation for their original family estate, which a Hohenzollern elector had coveted and seized. The Bismarcks had done nothing to gain distinction during their long feudal obscurity. Ferdinand did not even exert himself to fight for his king. He left the Prussian army at 23; and missed both the disastrous Jena campaign in 1806 and the War of Liberation against Napoleon in 1813. The efficient management of his rambling estates was beyond him, and he drifted helplessly into economic difficulties. It needed a vivid imagination for the son to turn this easygoing, slow-witted man, with his enormous frame, into a hero, representing all that was best in Prussian tradition.

Wilhelmine, the mother, was a different character. Her family, the Menkens, were bureaucrats without a title, not aristocrat landowners. Some of them had been university professors. Her father was a servant of the Prussian state, prized by Frederick the Great and later in virtual control of all home affairs. His reforms and quick critical spirit brought down on him the accusation of "Jacobinism." Wilhelmine was a town-child, at home only in the drawing rooms of Berlin. She had a sharp, restless intellect, which roamed without system from Swedenborg to Mesmer. At one moment she would be discussing the latest works of political liberalism; at the next dabbling in spiritualist experiments. Married to Ferdinand von Bismarck at sixteen, she developed interest neither for her heavy husband nor in country life. All her hopes were centered on her children. They were to achieve the intellectual life that had been denied to her. Her only ambition, she said, was to have "a grown-up son who would penetrate far further into the world of ideas than I, as a woman, have been able to do."

She gave her children encouragement without love. She drove them on; she never showed them affection. Otto, the younger son, inherited her brains. He was not grateful for the legacy. He wanted love from her, not ideas; and he was resentful that she did not share his admiration for his father. It is a psychological commonplace for a son to feel affection for his mother and to wish his father out of the way. The results are more interesting and more profound when a son, who takes after his mother, dislikes her character and standards of value. He will seek to turn himself into the father with whom he has little in common, and he may well end up neurotic or a genius. Bismarck was both. He was the clever, sophisticated son of a clever, sophisticated mother, masquerading all his life as his heavy, earthy father.

Even his appearance showed it. He was a big man, made bigger by his persistence in eating and drinking too much. He walked stiffly, with the upright carriage of a hereditary officer. Yet he had a small, fine head; the delicate hands of an artist; and when he spoke, his voice, which one would have expected to be deep and powerful, was thin and reedy — almost a falsetto — the voice of an academic, not of a man of action. Nor did he always present the same face to the world. He lives in history clean-shaven, except for a heavy mustache. Actually he wore a full beard for long periods of his life; and this at a time when beards were symbols on the continent of Europe of the romantic movement, if not of radicalism. In the use of a razor, as in other things, Bismarck sometimes followed Metternich, sometimes Marx. Despite his Junker mien, he had the sensitivity of a woman, incredibly quick in responding to the moods of another, or even in anticipating them. His conversational charm could bewitch tsars, queens and revolutionary leaders. Yet his great strokes of policy came after long solitary brooding, not after discussion with others. Indeed he never exchanged ideas in the usual sense of the term. He gave orders or, more rarely, carried them out; he did not cooperate. In a life of conflict, he fought himself most of all. He said once: "Faust complains of having two souls in his breast. I have a whole squabbling crowd. It goes on as in a republic." When someone asked him if he were really the Iron Chancellor, he replied: "Far from it. I am all nerves, so much so that self-control has always been the greatest task of my life and still is." He willed himself into a line of policy or action. His friend Keyserling noted of his conversion to religion: "Doubt was not fought and conquered; it was silenced by heroic will."

He felt himself always out of place, solitary and a stranger to his surroundings. "I have the unfortunate nature that everywhere I could be seems desirable to me, and dreary and boring as soon as I am there." He loathed the intellectual circles of Berlin to which his mother introduced him, and in 1848 said to a liberal politician: "I am a Junker and mean to have the advantages of that position." But the years he spent as a Junker, managing his estates, were the most miserable of his life; and when, as chancellor, he retired to his beloved countryside, he was happy only so long as the state papers continued to pour in on him. He spent the twenty-eight years of supreme power announcing his wish to relinquish it; yet no man has left office with such ill grace or fought so unscrupulously to recover it. He despised writers and literary men; yet only Luther and Goethe rank with him as masters of German prose. He found happiness only in his family; loved his wife, and gave to his children the affection that he had been denied by his mother. He said in old age that his greatest good fortune was "that God did not take any of my children from me." Yet he ruined the happiness of his adored elder son for the sake of a private feud, and thought nothing of spending a long holiday away from his wife in the company of a pretty girl; indeed he was so self-centered that he boasted to his wife of the girl's charm and good looks. He claimed to serve sometimes the king of Prussia, sometimes Germany, sometimes God. All three were cloaks for his own will; and he turned against them ruthlessly when they did not serve his purpose. He could have said with Oliver Cromwell, whom he much resembled: "He goeth furthest who knows not whither he is going." The young Junker had no vision that he would unify Germany on the basis of universal suffrage; and the maker of three wars did not expect to end as the great buttress of European peace.

Bismarck was not brought up as a Junker, despite his constant assertions of this character in later life. The family moved soon after he was born to the smaller estate of Kniephof in Pomerania. Here there was a smaller house with no architectural pretensions and hard practical farming. The Junkers, unlike the English gentry, did not live on rents. They worked the land themselves, and their peasants were, in reality, agricultural laborers, many of whom did not cultivate any land of their own. Bismarck experienced this idyllic existence only till he was seven. Then his mother set up house in Berlin, no doubt much to her own satisfaction, but ostensibly to send her sons to school in the capital. This exile from the country gave Bismarck a lasting grievance against his mother. The education which she chose for him was another. A Junker's son usually went into a cadet corps and, later, joined a cavalry regiment, even if he was not destined for a permanent military career. Wilhelmine, however, insisted that her children should have an intellectual education suited to the grandsons of the great Menken; and Bismarck went to the best Berlin grammar school of the day where he mixed with the sons of middle-class families. His mother revived her connections with the court; and Bismarck led a privileged existence, mixing on intimate terms with the younger Hohenzollerns. This counted in his later career. Despite his sturdy affectation of independence, he was always inside the royal circle and was treated as one of the family.

The spirit of the Enlightenment still dominated Prussian education; and Bismarck left school "as a Pantheist and if not as a republican, with the belief that a republic was the most reasonable form of state." His mother once more imposed her intellectual standards by sending him out of Prussia to the University of Göttingen in Hanover, the greatest liberal center of the day. Bismarck at first took a radical line. He defied university discipline both in behavior and ideas. What was more, he joined the *Burschenschaften* — students' unions which tried to keep alive the revolutionary spirit of the War of Liberation. He soon turned the other way. It was one thing to pose as a young radical in the court circles of Berlin; quite another to accept these ill-bred students from the middle class as his equals. Personal relations changed Bismarck's political outlook, as was often to happen in his later life. He suddenly discovered pride of blood and joined an aristocratic students-corps. He still led a disorderly existence. He drank a great deal; had some passionate *affaires*; and, like the young Disraeli, wore fantastic and colorful clothes. He was always ready for a duel, though the only time he was injured he characteristically alleged that it was a foul blow — an allegation which he maintained unforgivingly even thirty years later. After three terms, debts drove him back to Berlin, where he could live at home; and here he put in a second academic year. In May 1835, when he was just twenty, he scraped through the examination which qualified him for entry into the Prussian civil service.

Though Bismarck was never a great scholar, his years at the university left their mark. He read widely, despite his boasts of idleness, though he read more history than the law that he was supposed to be studying. He liked Schiller, admired Goethe, and ranked Shakespeare and Byron above either of them — tastes characteristic of the romantic movement. Scott was his greatest favorite of all, romance and history blended in the right proportions. Bismarck's classical learning was scanty; his scientific knowledge almost nonexistent. All the historical references in his speeches are to the three hundred years since the Reformation; his occasional echoes of Darwinism only what he could pick up from a newspaper. Philosophy never interested him; and he was one of the few Germans to escape the influence of Hegel. People were always more important to Bismarck than books. . . .

In 1844 he returned to the Prussian civil service, only to leave it again after a fortnight. His simple explanation was: "I have never been able to put up with superiors." By now he was 30, bitter, cynical and neurotic, his gifts running to nothing. New life came unexpectedly with religion, a wife, and a revolution. Bismarck learnt religion from the only neighbors for whom he cared — devout Lutherans who developed a quietist religion in a Quaker spirit. He was impressed by their content and peaceful confidence. Hoping to discover their secret, he spent much time in their company; and he found there a wife, Johanna von Puttkamer. His open avowal of religious belief was, no doubt, made partly to win her hand. After baring his soul to his prospective father-in-law, he wrote lightheartedly to his sceptical brother:

> I think I am entitled to count myself among the adherents of the Christian religion. Though in many doctrines, perhaps in those which they regard as essential, I am far removed from their standpoint, yet a sort of treaty . . . has been silently established between us. Besides, I like piety in women and have a horror of feminine cleverness.

This letter, too, was a piece of diplomacy, with its repudiation of their mother in the last sentence. Yet there can be no doubt that, whatever reserves he might have for his brother, Bismarck's faith became strong and sincere.

His religion was far removed from Christianity, or rather from the humanitarian Christianity of the twentieth century. There was in it little love, except for his own family. He believed in the God of the Old Testament and of the English puritans, the God of battles.

Luther or Oliver Cromwell would have understood Bismarck's religion, though it is less easily grasped by those for whom religion is simply a high-flown form of liberalism. Bismarck certainly used war as an instrument of policy and exercised secular power to the full. Anglo-Saxon sentimentalists are therefore inclined to suggest that his religion was sham. Yet the overwhelming majority of Christians have agreed with Bismarck in both theory and practice for nearly two thousand years. Lutheranism especially never claimed to lay down moral principles for public policy. It taught that service to the state and to the appointed ruler was a high religious duty. Bismarck felt this himself: "I believe that I am obeying God when I serve the king." His religion gave to his unstable personality a settled purpose and a sense of power. He said just after Sedan: "You would not have had such a chancellor if I had not the wonderful basis of religion." He believed that he was doing God's work in making Prussia strong and in unifying Germany. The belief itself brought power. God was on his side; therefore he could ignore the opposition of men. Like others who have had this belief, he easily persuaded himself that whatever suited him at the moment was God's purpose and, indeed, that he understood this purpose a great deal better than did God Himself.

Marriage brought to Bismarck lasting and secure happiness. Unlike most men, Bismarck did not marry his mother, but her opposite — a simple, devoted woman, endlessly patient and ready to put up with anything. Under his rough exterior, he was deeply emotional, a man of the romantic movement. He had grown up just when the Byronic legend dominated the Continent. He was the contemporary of Heine and Wagner. Like Gladstone, he was much given to tears at any public or private crisis; no doubt he too would have wept over *East Lynne*. He broke down sobbing after his first public speech and again after the battle of Sadowa. He wept when he became prime minister and even more when he left office. William I and he often sobbed together, though Bismarck always got his way. Music affected him deeply, the more because he could neither play nor read it. And by music he meant a soft glow of feeling when the sonatas of Beethoven were played with more expression than accuracy. He agreed with his wife's verdict on Anton Rubinstein, the greatest pianist of the age: "The playing was masterly both in control and attack and in everything you like, and yet 'the heart, the heart remains homeless.' " Johanna gave him a home for his heart, and it was very homely indeed. Though he played high drama on the public stage, his private setting resembled a Victorian boarding-house. Even in that tasteless age contemporaries commented on the banality of Bismarck's surroundings.

Bismarck as Prime Minister. Bismarck is portrayed in this lithograph as he appeared in 1863, in his late forties, soon after becoming head of the cabinet in Berlin. The expression on his face suggests his readiness to end the constitutional conflict in Prussia by "blood and iron." (Archiv für Kunst und Geschichte, Berlin)

II Tamer of Parliament

Heinrich von Sybel

The Great Compromise

Among the Prussian liberals who first opposed Bismarck and then supported him was the prominent historian Heinrich von Sybel. He was
rewarded for his loyal service to the united Germany by being asked to
write the semiofficial history of its establishment. The result was the
seven volumes of *The Founding of the German Empire by William I.*
Despite its title, the hero of the work is not the ruler but his minister.
One wit even suggested that there was a misprint in the name of the
book, that it should be "notwithstanding" instead of "by." Bismarck
is portrayed as the soul of moderation and compromise. A critic
complained that Sybel had transformed the tiger into a pussycat. In the

Source: From Heinrich von Sybel, *The Founding of the German Empire by William I,*
7 vols. (New York, 1890–1898), V:390–391, 404–409, 487–491.

following selection he describes the political consequences of the Prussian victory at Sadowa on July 3, 1866.

The 3d of July had brought the Prussian government, not only the overwhelming victory over Austria, but also a telling success against the opposition at home. At the same time that the Prussian battalions were annihilating the Austrian army, the opposition suffered such losses in the elections to the Parliament that the government, whose party in the years of the constitutional struggle had at times melted away to ten or twelve members, carried through their candidates for nearly half of the Lower House. With such a combination of political and military triumphs how many of the great conquerors of ancient or modern times would have resisted the temptation to break in pieces the hostile empire without, and to propose to themselves the overthrow of all constitutional restraints within.

But Bismarck was made of other stuff. He was not striving for world-dominion nor for boundless power, but for the means to secure and strengthen his Prussian Fatherland. So much acquisition of power and of territory as was necessary for this he laid hold of with iron grasp — so much and no more. The intoxication of victory never disordered his judgment, nor got the mastery over his fixed principles of moderation. . . .

The opening of the Parliament was fixed for Sunday noon, August 5th, in the celebrated white hall of the royal palace; and it can easily be imagined with what intense suspense the appearance of the king was awaited. Every one said to himself that the old struggle over the organization of the army had been ended upon the battlefields of Bohemia: whoever might still have wished to dispute the intrinsic value of that creation of King William's would have exposed himself to everlasting ridicule. But who knew what further use the king would make of this triumph? The men of the *Kreuzzeitung* party threatened, and those of the Party of Progress feared, that now a budgetless rule would be proclaimed to be the only proper system, and any further opposition would be put down by a dictatorship that had become allpowerful. The whole existence of the constitution seemed to tremble in the balance.

Accordingly, on the 5th of August, every one that could offer any claim whatever to the right to enter the palace sought to gain admission. All the galleries and boxes around the hall were filled to overflowing, and the members of the two Houses were present in unusual numbers. Soon after twelve o'clock the royal procession arrived; and at the appearance of the king the excited state of public feeling manifested itself in tremendous cheers.

The king, with the heir apparent on his right and the ministers on his left, took his place in front of the throne and began with a loud voice, amidst the breathless stillness of the audience, to read the speech. The first clause expressed thanks for God's gracious guidance; and accompanying the especial mention of the heroic deeds and terrible sacrifices of the nation in arms came the admonition that a harmonious cooperation of the government and the popular representation might bring to maturity the fruits whose seeds had been so bedewed with blood. The state of the finances, the king continued, was brilliant; it had been possible, without extraordinarily burdening the people, to bring the great war to a glorious conclusion. During the last year or so, indeed, an agreement as to the budget had not been arrived at. The public outlay during that time had therefore lacked that legal authorization, which, as was often admitted, the department of finance could receive only from the law passed every year and agreed upon between the government and the representatives of the people. Under these circumstances, the government had felt itself obliged, without such a law, to make such disbursements as were indispensable to the maintenance of the state; its conduct had been the result of an unavoidable necessity, such as a government, in the interest of the country, could not and might not seek to evade. It was, however, to be hoped that in view of recent events the indemnity which the government was about to move would be readily voted; and that thus the conflict that had been kept up hitherto would be terminated for all time; all the more surely was this to be expected since it was believed that the political condition of the Fatherland would permit an enlargement of the boundaries of the state and the establishment of a unified confederate army under the leadership of Prussia.

Though the satisfactory contents and the warm tone of the speech had already occasioned more than once an expression of approval among the hearers, at this point the inward, inspiring sense of freedom from anxiety that was felt by the immense majority of the spectators burst forth in loud and renewed applause. So there was to be no *coup d'état,* no overthrowal of the constitution! The prospect was held out of the restoration of internal peace, not by military authority, but by a simple harmonious settlement: the Lower House recognizing on its part its error in judgment, now so clearly proven, with regard to the new organization of the army, and the crown on its side recognizing anew and confirming the right of the House to determine the budget. The heaviest burden was thus removed from the bosoms of thousands of patriotic men. Now let a foreign disturber of the peace dare to cross the frontier!

The king concluded his speech with these words, which he had added on his own account to the original draft:

> *Gentlemen! You feel, and the whole Fatherland feels with me, the great importance of the moment which has brought me back among you again. May Providence as graciously bless Prussia in the future as it has visibly done in the immediate past. God grant it may be so!*

According to custom, the president of the Upper House answered the royal speech with a thrice repeated *vivat* for the king, in which the assembly joined with a veritable storm of enthusiasm. All hearts were touched. And who could have resisted the impression of the power and the benignity that were stamped on the countenance of the aged ruler?

That the Lower House would not reject the hand that was proffered to it was evident at the very opening of its sessions. During the whole continuance of the constitutional struggle, the president had been Grabow, a man by no means of radically democratic tendencies, but passionately excited by the violation of his sense of right. He had frequently from the presidential chair given violent expression to his convictions concerning the unconstitutional course pursued by the government. He now with noble self-abnegation expressed to the House his desire that his re-election should not be considered, so that his name might not be an obstacle in the way of reconciliation.

Thereupon, Von Forckenbeck, the candidate of the parties that had hitherto constituted the opposition, was elected by 170 votes against 136 of the Conservatives and 22 of the Old Liberals. There was therefore now, as before, no ministerial party with a certain majority; but, nevertheless, the election of Forckenbeck proclaimed the victory of moderate tendencies and conciliatory principles even in the circles of modern and advanced liberalism. For in the very beginning of the constitutional struggle Forckenbeck, by bringing up motions for amendment and for conciliation, had stood in marked contrast with the purely negative attitude of Waldeck and his associates. The election of such a man was the first symptom of a new formation of parties with a tendency at once liberal and national.

Violent and bitter as the feeling had been during the conflict, it was no longer possible not to see that the government and the Liberals were pursuing the same object, and that for the normal establishment of the German state the power of the government was quite as needful as the general agitation of public sentiment. Whoever was in earnest on the subject of German unity was bound to declare himself, willingly or unwillingly, an ally of the government in the question which controlled the whole life of Germany; and, consequently, whoever was in earnest about the practical realization of liberal ideas was bound to make up his mind to cooperate actively with the government, in order not to leave the new arrangement of the German state entirely to his political opponents. For four years the constitutional struggle had united the great mass of the Liberals with the Radical Democrats, and had thus cut off the former from any share in the furtherance of the German cause. From the moment when circumstances rendered possible the settlement of that constitutional struggle, this unnatural alliance began to be dissolved. Independent of the Radical groups there arose once more a Liberal party, now brought upon the side of the government by the German question, but at the same time independent in its principles, and soon to grow largely in numbers and in influence. . . .

The government had already, on the 14th of August, sent to the House the draft of an indemnity bill, containing the motion to grant to the ministry of state indemnity for the expenses incurred during the years 1862–1865, a general outline of which was appended; while for the year 1866, since the state of things was no longer adapted to the establishment of a regular budget, the government desired a loan of 154 million thalers. In the budget committee, to whose consideration the matter was referred, it was very soon evident that a large majority favored the acceptance of the bill.

The only determined opposition came from the members of the Party of Progress, who were not able to find in the draft of the bill the necessary security for the reestablishment of constitutional rights. These, therefore, approved the loan for 1866, but wished to decline for the present the proposal about the indemnity and to leave it with the government to make the request again after the budget for 1867 should have been fixed upon.

To this the reply was made that if the present promise of the government to adopt the budget for 1867 were not to be trusted, then the passage and adoption of this latter could not be looked upon as a sure guaranty for the acceptance of a regular budget for 1868. The main thing, it was asserted, was the serious intention of the government to return to the basis of the constitution; and this determination was believed to be sufficiently indicated in the bill. The whole dispute arose, it was said, from a difference of opinion about the new organization of the army, and who could at this late day think of undertaking any essential changes in the same? For, indeed, it was very probable that if it had been possible to foresee the last war and its consequences, the House would not have thought of refusing its approval to the new military constitution. The matter of the organization of the army must be settled anew, it was argued, by a definite law; but such a law would not under the existing state of things have to be passed by the Prussian Lower House but by the North German Parliament. The report revised by Deputy Twesten in accordance with these sentiments was adopted by the committee by a vote of twenty-five to eight.

In the House the discussion was, as ever, more lively, and the views more sharply opposed to one another. The whole Party of Progress set themselves determinedly against the bill. Waldeck considered that nothing whatever had been offered that justified any expectation of more constitutional conduct on the part of the government. Schultze-Delitzsch declared that the whole war had been carried on not only without the consent, but even against the will, of the Prussian people; and he was naive enough to refer to those melancholy addresses of peace of May and June as a brilliant proof of Prussia's careful prudence compared with the tumult of war which prevailed then at Vienna.

Virchow explained that he and his friends had known a better way leading to German unity than Bismarck's, namely, the way of freedom. But as things now stood, he said, they were willing to sacrifice their wishes to Bismarck, and were willing to support his foreign policy, but must so much the more energetically defend constitutional rights. As if Benedek in June would have allowed himself to be deterred from marching upon Berlin by the fiery enthusiasm of the Party of Progress for freedom! or as if there could have been at this time any worse foe to Bismarck's German policy conceivable than the continuance of the internal quarrel! The professor of Catholic theology, Michelis, supplemented these remarks by the brilliant observation that Tetzel in 1517 was accused unjustly for having sold indulgences for future sins, but that this bill did indeed involve a pardon for all the future sins of the ministry.

The Conservative party, delighted at the favorable sentiments, declared with great ardor that it would vote for the indemnity-bill in accordance with the wishes of the government, although strictly speaking, something entirely different would be more properly in order, namely, a hearty vote of thanks to the government for not having taken account of the foolish behavior of the House. The mediatory position held by Bismarck and Von der Heydt also received eloquent support from the parties of the Center. Lasker and Georg Vincke, at other times seldom to be found on the same side, and also, at the close of the discussion, Twesten, who had made the report, demonstrated with convincing force the importance of the present situation, the consequence of a continued quarrel with the government, and the power of public opinion which demanded unity of action.

The final vote on the report resulted in 230 in favor and 75 against, the latter including the Party of Progress, some few members of the Left Center, and the Catholic fraction. The Upper House followed this example on the 8th of September, after Herr von Kleist-Retzow had given vent to his regrets at the injurious compliance on the part of the government. The vote of the Upper House resulted in the unanimous acceptance of the bill as drawn up by the House of Deputies.

Internal peace was thus secured and the four years' contest over the constitution was ended. With good practical sense, that question which lay at the very bottom of the quarrel, namely, what was to happen if again sometime the budget should not be passed, was left to future decision; and it was considered sufficient to heal the present wound by mutually trusting to the royal word: "It will not happen again."

Since then more than twenty years have passed. Often enough have the representatives of the people refused to pass bills presented by the government; but they have never found any reason to doubt the loyalty of the ministers to the constitution. It has not happened again. And may it not happen again, that the popular representation on its part shall occasion such an urgent condition of things that the welfare of the state shall be the only law in force!

Otto Pflanze

Liberalism Surrenders

Not all scholars agree that the reconciliation of crown and parliament in Prussia in 1866 represented the triumph of sweet reasonableness over dogmatism and partisanship. Otto Pflanze, a well-known American historian, suggests in his learned and discerning biography of Bismarck that the liberals lost more than they won by approving the bill of indemnity. They may have thought that by their capitulation they would gain the opportunity to participate in the creation of a new civic order in their country. In fact they sacrificed their principles for a mess of pottage, for a spurious parliamentarism and an egocentric nationalism. Their surrender to success helped reinforce the tradition of authority in Germany that led to war and defeat in the twentieth century.

On August 5, 1866, the white hall of the palace, so empty on February 23, was crowded with deputies, the political atmosphere completely changed. Popular support, for which the opposition had angled so long, was now overwhelmingly on the side of the monarchy. The army, whose reorganization they had opposed and whose finan-

Source: Otto Pflanze, *Bismarck and the Development of Germany, Vol. I: The Period of Unification, 1815–1871*, pp. 330–336. Copyright © 1990 by Princeton University Press.

cial support they had denied, was brilliantly victorious. Its officers were the Junkers against whose power they had striven in vain. Its commander-in-chief was the king whose ministers had violated the constitution and frustrated the parliamentary will. Back of the whole conservative order, furthermore, loomed the sentiment of German nationalism. In seven weeks dynasty, ministers, army, and Junkers had taken a mighty step toward the realization of the liberal dream of half a century. Achievement of the rest was assumed to be but a matter of time. Now the government announced its willingness to seek a settlement of the constitutional conflict.

The situation was powerfully persuasive. That liberals were so strongly affected by it, however, cannot be attributed merely to the dramatic events of June and July 1866. Their acquiescence had been prepared for more than a century in the development of the liberal tradition.... German moderate liberals had always had an ambivalent attitude toward the state, an attitude that reflected the intermediate character of their position in German society. Their value system was that of the German *Mittelstand*, suspended between the traditional ruling estates (*Adelsstand* and *Beamtenstand*) of the Prussian establishment, which liberals aspired to join rather than replace, and (at this stage in the evolution of Germany's economy and society) the inchoate *Volk*, whose potential for disorder they had learned to fear. As in 1848 they were leery of the masses, and as in 1848 the masses were not behind them. With few exceptions, they had never aimed at full responsibility for the management of public affairs. During the constitutional conflict they had fought a largely defensive action in behalf of the *Rechtsstaat* and against arbitrary government. What Bismarck now offered could be interpreted as victory, not defeat.

In early 1864 many liberals had displayed a hunger for military success and foreign expansion; now they found this but an appetizer for the main course. Theirs had been the illusion that wars for great objectives could be fought only with their active support. But now the unbelievable had happened. The supposed spokesman of reactionary conservatism had not only steered the country into a major war, but had also summoned the nation to accomplish its unity under the protective umbrella of Prussian power. Again the Prussian state had stolen vital planks from the liberal platform. To most there now appeared no other place to stand than upon or under the inviting new structure Bismarck was busily erecting with stolen materials.

For many the conversion was not difficult. Wehrenpfennig concluded, "Bismarck is, except for Stein, the greatest statesman Prussia has ever had; it appears that he is luckier and perhaps even bolder than the latter." Rudolf Ihering, Göttingen professor of law, who earlier had denounced the war as an act of "frightful frivolity," now bowed down before the "genius of a Bismarck," declaring that for such a man of deeds he would give one hundred men of impotent honesty. Almost overnight the Bismarck cult was born. Its devotees began to reinterpret their hero's actions during the preceding four years. They excused his infringements of the constitution in view of what was presumed to have been his hidden purpose. Impatiently the liberal press, so bitterly hostile from March to June, now pressed the deputies not to hinder the government in the fulfillment of its "duty" toward the rest of Germany. In view of the "glorious" work ahead, the issues of the constitutional conflict were declared petty and insignificant.

The classic conversions were those of Gustav Mevissen and Hermann Baumgarten. After watching the victorious columns march down Unter den Linden through the Brandenburger Tor, Mevissen, who had headed the revolutionary cabinet of 1848, described the emotions that gripped him: "I cannot shake off the impression of this hour. I am no devotee of Mars; I feel more attached to the goddess of beauty and the mother of graces than to the mighty god of war, but the trophies of war exercise a magic charm upon the child of peace. One's eyes are involuntarily riveted on, and one's spirit goes along with, the unending rows of men who acclaim the god of the moment — success." Baumgarten — student of Gervinus, press official of the new era, professor of history at Karlsruhe — subjected the attitudes of German liberals to a scorching "self-criticism" in the pages of the *Preussische Jahrbücher.* Theoretical and doctrinaire, they had placed their faith in words and ideas, not deeds. Recent events had shown that the German Mittelstand could not dispense with the leadership of a "true aristocracy" for the achievement of national objectives. Liberals must abandon their oppositional posture.

With care Bismarck nourished the plant of liberal capitulation. Soon after the Landtag opened he fed the deputies a series of bills designed to appeal to every segment of the former opposition. For men of principle there was a bill of indemnity, for Prussian chauvinists a bill of annexation, for German nationalists a Reichstag suffrage bill. He appeared in person to defend and explain them before the committees; in private talks he spun the web of personal charm and sweet reason that had snared so many diplomatic opponents. When the situation called for it, the master of scorn and contempt was equally adept at deference and consideration. He enjoyed the game intensely. A visitor reported that his face, while pale and ill, was radiant with laughter. The man was beyond all exaggeration.

After Königgrätz liberal deputies were greatly relieved to learn that the triumphant Junker did not intend a coup against the constitution and that he was still serious about a national parliament. Their first chance to respond to his overtures was in the election of a speaker. Since 1862 Grabow had annually been reelected to that office and his bitter opening speeches had been the first demonstration in each parliamentary session of the continued intransigence of the opposition. But now the deputies chose Forckenbeck, a moderate noted for tact and parliamentary skill. In drafting a reply to the speech from the throne, the moderates allowed amendments that made it acceptable even to conservatives. They argued that the message must demonstrate that the German people were entirely united behind the German policy of the government. Only twenty-five deputies voted against it, including the veteran radical Jacoby, who once more condemned the war as a blow to freedom.

Already there were signs of dissolution in the liberal ranks. In mid-August a left centrist, Karl Kannegiesser, reported to his constituents, "The world-historical events of the last months are having a powerful effect upon men's minds." He detected two currents in both of the major liberal parties: one placed the major emphasis on the German question, the other upon Prussian constitutional law. Relieved of the pressure of the constitutional conflict and presented with the possibility of national unity under authoritarian auspices, liberal deputies began to divide once more into the two traditional segments of moderate right and democratic left. The alliance of 1861 broke apart over the issue of the relative importance of national unity and the rule of law.

Both camps, to be sure, were inclined toward settlement. But moderates considered the constitutional conflict irretrievably lost and wished to get rid of it on the government's terms; democrats were inclined to seek as firm a guarantee as possible for the future respect of parliament's budget rights. The men of the left found it difficult to join the general jubilation. They had not forgotten that the last breach of the constitution — the creation by decree of a system of credit banks — had occurred but months before the indemnity bill. They noted that even now the minister of interior continued his "disciplinary" measures against liberal officials and his refusal to confirm liberal city councillors; the minister of justice persisted in his prosecution of the liberal press and opposition deputies (including Twesten). Finally, they observed that the government's indemnity bill contained no guarantee against budgetless rule in the future. When Forckenbeck officially presented the chamber's address, Wilhelm responded belligerently, "I had to act that way, and I shall do so again, if the same circumstances recur."

In the great debate on the indemnity bill leaders of the left — Waldeck, Gneist, Ziegler, Virchow, Hoverbeck, Jacoby, Frentzel, and Schulze-Delitzsch — maintained that its passage would legitimize the "gap theory" and pardon four years of unconstitutional behavior on the part of the cabinet. The deputies should postpone the bill pending passage of a legal budget and a law fixing ministerial responsibility. Military victory and respect for law must not be confused with each other. Whatever its successes abroad, the government must stay within the law at home. But leaders of the right — Twesten, Forckenbeck, Lasker, and Michaelis — feared that, if liberals remained in opposition, the flight of the voters to the conservatives would continue. By supporting the Bismarck cabinet, on the other hand, they might sever it from its conservative base and influence the future constitutional structure of Germany. In summing up the moderate position, Twesten declared that two issues were fundamental to every state: those of freedom and power. "No one may be criticized for giving precedence to the issue of power at this time and maintaining that the issues of freedom can wait, provided that nothing happens that can permanently prejudice them." From Bismarck the deputies heard of the dangers of French intervention and Austrian resurgence. Only a united people could succeed in Germany's mission against an injured and envious Europe. On September 3, 1866, the indemnity bill passed by a vote of 230 to 75.

The constitutional conflict was over, but so also was the unity of the liberal movement. During August and September the caucuses of the Progressive party became increasingly heated. The exodus of the moderates began with Michaelis, followed by Twesten, Lasker, and many others. By a number of concessions Bismarck gave the secessionists the chance to feel at last the exhilaration of being in harmony with the ruling power. They were permitted to redraft the indemnity bill to make it correspond with the budget clauses of the constitution. Instead of "personal union," Bismarck accepted the actual incorporation of the conquered lands into Prussia, but inauguration of the Prussian constitution was to be delayed one year. A bill presented by Heydt to legalize the government-sponsored credit banks was passed, but only after an amendment that soon put them out of business. A serious clash over the government's request for a credit of 60 million thalers was settled by a compromise that limited the size and purpose of the reserves accumulated by the treasury. Prodded by Lasker and Forckenbeck, the crown issued a general amnesty on September 21, the day of the victory celebration in Berlin. Wilhelm's request for a donation of one and a half million thalers for victorious generals was voluntarily amended by the chamber to include the name of Bismarck!

Originally, the secessionists did not intend to found a new party. Their aim was to convince the majority in the Left Center and Progressive parties of the validity of a new strategy. Some of them saw in Bismarck's foreign policy a significant gain for liberty in Germany. The exclusion of Catholic Austria from a unified Germany under Protestant leadership was itself a liberal deed, a victory for modernity over clerical bigotry. By supporting the Bismarck cabinet in foreign affairs, moreover, they hoped to bring it step by step along the road of domestic compromise; constitutional issues should be postponed issues until they could be fought out on more advantageous terrain. In the expanded Landtag and constituent Reichstag of 1867 the secessionists found many non-Prussian liberals sympathetic to their cause. Never personally involved in the Prussian conflict, the latter were untainted by its passions and less concerned about its issues. They too regarded the struggle as lost and relatively unimportant compared to the great task ahead. Out of this union of forces came the National Liberal party. In numbers non-Prussians predominated, and the leadership fell to two Hanoverians, Bennigsen and Miquel.

The liberal caucus in the Chamber of Deputies had divided between a Progressive party, largely Prussian and preserving the tradition of the conflict years, and a National Liberal party, largely non-Prussian and more national than liberal. Economic issues, such as the recent renewal of the Zollverein on the basis of free trade, appear to have had no influence on the split. And yet the two parties, because of the positions their leaders took on many economic and political issues, did tend to attract different segments of the German *Mittelstand*. The priority given to national unity by the moderate liberals who formed the National Liberal party appealed to many merchants, industrialists, liberal landowners, and their journalistic supporters. They saw in the erection of a political roof over the national marketplace a significant gain for bourgeois interests. But they also found merit in Bismarck's argument that Prussia was compelled to carry too great a military and financial burden for the defense of Germany as a whole; a united Germany under Prussian leadership could be expected to spread the tax burden proportionally to other shoulders and in the long run free capital for more productive purposes. To the small businessmen and artisans of democratic temperament who clung to the Progressive party the financial benefits to be expected of German unity were either less important or not so apparent; hence they were more reluctant than the moderates to surrender or defer the issues of freedom and parliamentary rights for which the constitutional conflict had been fought.

To the democratic left the cleavage was between "opportunists" and "men of principle"; to the moderate right it was between "practical statesmen" and "naive idealists." And yet the formation of two separate caucuses in parliament did not mean that the liberal movement as a whole was vertically cloven apart in 1867. For at least a decade the tradition remained alive that there was but one "liberal party" with a common social and electoral base, the *Mittelstand*. Nor was this mere theory in the Chamber of Deputies (later the Reichstag), where the two caucuses collaborated on many basic issues, and in the provinces and electoral districts, where liberals were often chosen as candidates without regard to parliamentary affiliations. Still, German liberalism had reached a point of divergence. The moderates took the track that ultimately led to unconditional surrender, the democrats that which finally ended in frustration and impotence.

Erich Eyck

The Subverter of Freedom

One of the most important revisionist biographies of Bismarck appeared appropriately enough during World War II. Its author was Erich Eyck, a German lawyer and historian who was forced to seek refuge in England from persecution by the National Socialists. An admirer of the British liberal tradition, he condemned the Iron Chancellor for stifling the growth of representative institutions in Central Europe. He was sharply attacked by those historians among whom the Bismarck cult was still strong. But his work was on the whole a healthy antidote to the hero worship usually accorded the unifier of Germany. The selection that follows describes the period of constitutional conflict in Prussia, which began in 1862.

Bismarck's appointment made a great but on the whole a very unfavorable impression. The London *Spectator* called him the most outspoken Junker who had ever ruled in Prussia, and a man of strong but limited understanding. The German, and particularly the Prussian, Liberals felt that a great struggle was ahead. One of the leaders of the Progressive Party wrote:

> *Bismarck, that is to say: government without budget, rule by the sword in home affairs, and war in foreign affairs. I consider him the most dangerous minister for Prussia's liberty and happiness.*

This expressed the popular feeling rather accurately. In the theaters, every malicious allusion to the king was received with a storm of applause.

Source: Erich Eyck, *Bismarck and the German Empire*, 2/e, 1968, pp. 58–63, The Macmillan Press Ltd.

Bismarck's first task was to form his cabinet. The foreign minister, Count Bernstorff, and the minister of finance, von der Heydt, again declined to govern unconstitutionally without a budget and retired from the government. At first Bismarck tried to make contact with moderate Liberals. For instance, he asked Twesten, the mover of the compromise amendment, to see him. Bismarck did not have strong views about the length of military service. For his own person he would have accepted the two years' period; but as the king was opposed to it there was nothing he was able to offer to Twesten. So the interview came to nothing. It is remarkable, anyhow, for the rather startling and indiscreet way in which Bismarck talked to this member of the Opposition about the king who just had appointed him. He compared the king with a horse that shied at every new object and became restive and unmanageable if one tried force, but would get accustomed to it little by little.

Bismarck never had the serious intention of taking a Liberal into his cabinet. As a matter of fact, he composed it of reactionary officials who had no other merit than their conservative opinions and their noble birth. In later years Bismarck spoke of most of them in the most depreciating and disdainful way. The finance minister, von Bodelschwingh, he calls "a liar," and the agricultural minister, von Selchow, an ass (*Rindvieh*). Only the minister of the interior, Graf Eulenburg, was a man of gifts, though idle and frivolous. However insignificant these Junkers were, they met the two requirements for which Bismarck wanted ministers: they were all ready to help him to crush the Opposition and to let him make his foreign policy without putting any obstacles in his way.

In parliament, Bismarck began his activities by withdrawing the budget for the next year. Asked in the committee of the House what he proposed to do next, he made a speech which caused the greatest sensation. He took from his pocketbook an olive-branch — it was the olive-branch Katherine Orloff had given him when they parted in Avignon — showed it to the members of the committee with the words that it had been his intention to offer it to the House as a token of peace, but that he had now reluctantly come to the conclusion that it was still too early. He then spoke about Prussia's present situation and future task. Germany did not look, he said, to the liberalism of Prussia but to her power. Unfortunately, her frontiers were unfavorable to a healthy state. The great questions of the time could not be solved by speeches and majority votes — that was the great mistake of 1848 and 1849 — but by *blood and iron.*

The sensation these startling sentences made was the very reverse of favorable. Even Roon grew angry about these "racy excursions," which did not help in any way. The historian Heinrich von Treitschke, later the most outspoken prophet of Bismarck, raged about the ridiculous vulgarity of this shallow Junker boasting of the blood and iron with which he wanted to subjugate Germany. The king was not gratified either. He was in Baden at the time in the company of the queen, their daughter, the grand duchess of Baden, and their son-in-law, the grand duke. Bismarck knew that none of them was his friend, and he was afraid that they would turn his words against him. To win back the king, he met him in the train at the last station before Berlin, Jüterbog. Of this episode Bismarck has given a masterly description in his *Recollections* (chapter 12).

Whatever the king may have thought about Bismarck's utterances, he knew that he was indispensable for dealing with the chamber. In the great debate which arose there, and in which moderate and radical members alike refuted Bismarck's constitutional arguments, one of the moderate speakers, the famous lawyer, Professor Gneist, emphasized the point of principle. He warned the minister to respect an elementary quality of the German people: its belief in a firm moral and legal order as the last and decisive factor in the history of states. Gneist was right. Such was then, indeed, the feeling of the most important section of the Prussian people. The great question was whether this belief in the decisive power of the legal and moral order would be justified by events.

At first, developments took quite the opposite turn. The budget voted by the Chamber of Deputies was thrown out by the feudal Chamber of Seigneurs (Herrenhaus) and the government ruled without a budget. It continued to collect taxes and duties and to spend the collected money for military purposes quite arbitrarily. As it was a period of flourishing economic life, the yield of the taxes increased, so that the government was not embarrassed owing to want of money. The chamber was unable to stop this process. It lacked the legal means either to stop the collection of the taxes or to impeach the government. The constitution declared that the ministers were responsible, but it did not open a way for their impeachment if they broke the constitution. Therefore, the power of the

Chamber of Deputies was weak. Foreign critics failed to understand this position. English journals, for instance, often ascribed to lack of firmness in the Opposition what was, in fact, a weakness in its constitutional power.

How deeply Bismarck's methods offended the sense of justice of the German people came to light in the debate of the Chamber of Deputies on the address in January 1863. The official speaker of the committee of the House was the famous historian, Heinrich von Sybel, the same historian who under the auspices of Bismarck afterwards wrote his *History of the Foundation of the German Empire by William I*. He was not at all a radical, but a warm admirer of Prussia and her history. Sybel said:

> *The Ministers and the majority of this House speak a different language; their thoughts are ruled by a different logic and their actions by different moral laws.*

But the climax of the debate came when Bismarck bluntly told the House:

> *If a compromise cannot be arrived at and a conflict arises, then the conflict becomes a question of power. Whoever has the power, then acts according to his opinion.*

It was not a radical but the moderate Count Schwerin, a former minister of King William during the "New Era," who answered with these words:

> *The sentence in which the speech of the Prime Minister culminated: that "Might before Right," that "you may talk as you like, we have the power and will therefore force through our theory" — this is not a sentence which can support the dynasty of Prussia in the long run. The sentence on which the greatness of our dynasty and of our country rests, and the reverence which Prussia's sovereigns have enjoyed and will enjoy for ever and ever, is quite the reverse: "Right before Might."*

These words made a deep impression, and Count Schwerin was hailed as the defender of the good old Prussian tradition.

Bismarck defied the chamber, as the young William Pitt, in 1783, defied Charles Fox and the majority of the House of Commons. Both relied on their king. But there was a very important difference. Pitt knew that the voters, or those who directed the voters, were on his side, that he only had to bide his time to dissolve parliament in order to get a favorable majority. Bismarck knew that the people were even more passionately against him than the chamber. Time and again he dissolved the chamber: the voters always elected the same majority. All the vehement and often illegal pressure of the government did not succeed in making them vote for governmental candidates. The Prussian Opposition in the years 1862–1866 is, indeed, the only one in the whole history of constitutional Germany which could effectively depend upon their voters. In later years, 1878, 1887, 1893, 1907, a dissolution always gave the government the majority it wanted, because enough voters deserted the oppositional deputies. Only in the time of the Prussian constitutional conflict did they stick invariably to their guns. True, they voted according to the three-classes-suffrage, and the middle-class voters of the two first classes decided the election. But there can be no doubt that the majority of the workers in the third class sympathized fully with them. . . .

A government that encroaches on the constitution at one point, cannot stop there. It is forced by circumstances and by its own action from one illegality to another. The next point of attack was the freedom of the press, guaranteed by the constitution. The great majority of the newspapers was Liberal and supported the Opposition energetically. Bismarck tried to suppress them by an order of the king in June 1863, which empowered the police to suppress oppositional papers. By dissolving the chamber he managed to silence the press during the election. Nevertheless, the Opposition was again victorious at the polls and the order had to be cancelled after having been in force for five months.

This royal order against the press had a startling effect in an unexpected quarter. The heir to the throne, the crown prince, openly declared his opposition to it. The crown prince and his wife, Victoria, did not by any means approve of Bismarck's methods. They objected to his encroachments on the constitution and were afraid that they would open an insuperable gulf between the Prussian people and the dynasty. The prince warned the king against a breach of the constitution. The king had ordered him to attend the councils when he himself presided (*Kronrat*). But the decision to make the royal order against the press had been made when the prince was absent. He was on a tour of military inspection in the eastern provinces of the monarchy, when he suddenly learnt of the order for the first time by its publication in the press. On the advice of Princess Victoria, who accompanied him, and of the Liberal Chief Burgomaster of Danzig, Winter, he declared, answering a speech by Winter in the Danzig Town Hall: "I did not know anything of this order beforehand. I was absent. I am not one of those who advised it."

These words inevitably caused a tremendous sensation. The Prussian people was deeply moved by the open opposition of the heir to the throne; the king, on the other hand, was extremely angry and wrote his son a furious letter treating him, as Victoria wrote to her mother, like a little child. Victoria's letters, published by Sir Frederick Ponsonby in the *Letters of the Empress Frederick* and partly in the Second Series of the *Letters of Queen Victoria*, show the immensely difficult position in which the crown prince and his wife then found themselves. The Danzig episode became a decisive event in their lives. Bismarck never either forgot or forgave this opposition. Thus began the isolation of the princely couple, which from that time onwards cast a shadow over their lives. Bismarck's own point of view is given in his correspondence with the king, published in chapter 16 of *Reflections and Recollections*. His marginal notes on the memorandum of the prince state his case in a masterly manner. He based his arguments on the thesis that a crown prince did not have any official "status" and was therefore not entitled to play a political role and to make opposition to his father. But what would Bismarck himself have done if he had had a king whose policy he disliked, and a crown prince who supported him — in other words, if Frederick III had come to the throne, not struck down by his terrible and mortal malady but in full strength, and if his reign had lasted longer than merely ninety-nine short days? Fate has spared Bismarck this test. But whoever knows the story of those tragic ninety-nine days of 1888 will doubt whether Bismarck would have acted according to his doctrine of 1863.

Henry A. Kissinger

A Doomed Titan

Henry A. Kissinger, like Erich Eyck, was a refugee from Germany, a victim of Nazi ethnic bigotry; but unlike Eyck, he harbored no lasting bitterness toward the country of his birth. Coming to the United States as a young boy, Kissinger found it much easier to adapt to his new homeland. While teaching political science at Harvard University, shortly before he embarked on a new career in government service that was to culminate in his appointment in 1973 as U.S. secretary of state, he published a perceptive analysis of Bismarck's statecraft, portraying the architect of German unification as a political figure of extraordinary talent struggling in vain against the irresistible currents of his time. It is illuminating to read what a well-known *Realpolitiker* of the twentieth century has to say about an even better-known *Realpolitiker* of the nineteenth century.

Few statesmen have altered the history of their society so profoundly as Otto von Bismarck. Before he came to power, Prussia — and the rest of Germany — seemed to be undergoing the "normal" evolution toward parliamentary, constitutional rule. Indeed, the crisis that brought him to office in 1862 was the familiar issue of parliamentary control over the budget, which in every other West European country had been resolved in favor of parliament. Five years afterwards, Bismarck had changed the domestic orientation of Germany and the pattern of international relations by solving the issue of German unification which had baffled two generations. His solution had not occurred previously to any significant group or to any major political leader. Too democratic for conservatives, too authoritarian for liberals, too power-oriented for legitimists, the new order was tailored to a genius who proposed to restrain the

Source: Henry A. Kissinger, "The White Revolutionary: Reflections on Bismarck," reprinted by permission of *Daedalus,* Journal of the American Academy of Arts and Sciences, from the issue entitled "Philosophers and Kings: Studies in Leadership," Summer 1968, Vol. 97, No. 3, pp. 888–89, 918–22.

contending forces, both domestic and foreign, by manipulating their antagonisms.

"People are born as revolutionaries," the German liberal Bamberger wrote during his Parisian exile in 1862, as he attempted to explain the enigma of Bismarck's personality. "The accident of life decides whether one becomes a Red or a White revolutionary." Many years later Bismarck said that Bamberger was one of the few authors who had understood him.

What is a revolutionary? If the answer to this question were not ambiguous, few revolutionaries could succeed; the aims of revolutionaries seem self-evident only to posterity. This is sometimes due to deliberate deception. More frequently, it reflects a psychological failure: the inability of the "establishment" to come to grips with a fundamental challenge. The refusal to believe in irreconcilable antagonism is the reverse side of a state of mind to which basic transformations have become inconceivable. Hence, revolutionaries are often given the benefit of every doubt. Even when they lay down a fundamental theoretical challenge, they are thought to be overstating their case for bargaining purposes; they are believed to remain subject to the "normal" preferences for compromise. A long period of stability creates the illusion that change must necessarily take the form of a modification of the existing framework and cannot involve its overthrow. Revolutionaries always start from a position of inferior physical strength; their victories are primarily triumphs of conception or of will.

This is especially true when the challenge occurs not in the name of change, but by exposing institutions to strains for which they were not designed. Even the most avowedly conservative position can erode the political or social framework if it smashes its restraints; for institutions are designed for an average standard of performance — a high average in fortunate societies, but still a standard reducible to approximate norms. They are rarely able to accommodate genius or demoniac power. A society that must produce a great man in each generation to maintain its domestic or international position will doom itself; for the appearance and, even more, the recognition of a great man are to a large extent fortuitous.

The impact of genius on institutions is bound to be unsettling, of course. The bureaucrat will consider originality as unsafe, and genius will resent the constrictions of routine. In fortunate societies, a compromise occurs. Extraordinary performance may not be understood, but it is at least believed in (consider, for example, the British respect for eccentricity). Genius in turn will not seek fulfillment in rebellion. Stable societies have, therefore, managed to clothe greatness in the forms of mediocrity; revolutionary structures have attempted to institutionalize an attitude of exaltation. To force genius to respect norms may be chafing, but to encourage mediocrity to imitate greatness may produce institutionalized hysteria or complete irresponsibility.

This was the legacy of Bismarck. His was a strange revolution. It appeared in the guise of conservatism, yet the scale of its conception proved incompatible with the prevailing international order. It triumphed domestically through the vastness of its successes abroad. With a few brusque strokes Bismarck swept away the dilemmas that had baffled the German quest for unity. In the process, he recast the map of Europe and the pattern of international relations. Like the mythological figures Solon or Lycurgus, he created a society in his image and a community of nations animated by his maxims in their dealings with one another.

Everything about Bismarck was out of scale: his bulk and his appetite; his loves and even more his hatreds. The paradox of his accomplishments seemed embodied in his personality. The man of "blood and iron" wrote prose of extraordinary simplicity, plasticity, and power. The apostle of the claims of power was subject to fits of weeping in a crisis. The "Iron Chancellor" loved Shakespeare and copied pages of Byron in his notebook. The statesman who never ceased extolling reason of state possessed an agility of conception and a sense of proportion which, while he lived, turned power into an instrument of self-restraint.

But the gods sometimes punish pride by fulfilling man's wishes too completely. Statesmen who build lastingly transform the personal act of creation into institutions that can be maintained by an average standard of performance. This Bismarck proved incapable of doing. His very success committed Germany to a permanent tour de force. It created conditions that could be dealt with only by extraordinary leaders. Their emergence in turn was thwarted by the colossus who dominated his country for nearly a generation. Bismarck's tragedy was that he left a heritage of unassimilated greatness. . . .

[The] main lines of Bismarck's thought were established [by

1860]. One by one, he had attacked the assumptions on which the "Metternich system" was based. He had declared the German Confederation a fetter to the development of Prussia's power. He had seen in the Holy Alliance a means to perpetuate an unjustified subordination of Prussia to Austria. Austria, the traditional ally, had been asserted to be Prussia's antagonist and France, the "hereditary" enemy, was considered a potential ally. The unity of conservative interests, the truism of policy for over a generation, had been described as subordinate to the requirement of national interest. The state transcended its fleeting embodiments in various forms of government.

The significance of Bismarck's criticism did not, of course, reside in the fact that it was made — the tenuousness of the Metternich system was a shibboleth of the mid-nineteenth century — but in the manner by which it was justified. Heretofore the attacks on the principle of legitimacy had occurred in the name of other principles of presumably greater validity, such as nationalism or liberalism. Bismarck declared the relativity of *all* beliefs; he translated them into forces to be evaluated in terms of the power they could generate.

However hard-boiled Bismarck's philosophy appeared, it was also built on an article of faith no more demonstrable than the principle of legitimacy — the belief that decisions based on power would be constant, that a proper analysis of a given set of circumstances would necessarily yield the same conclusions for everybody. It was inconceivable to Gerlach that the principle of legitimacy was capable of various interpretations. It was beyond the comprehension of Bismarck that statesmen might differ in understanding the requirements of national interest. Because of his magnificent grasp of the nuances of power relationships, Bismarck saw in his philosophy a doctrine of self-limitation. Because these nuances were not apparent to his successors and imitators, the application of Bismarck's lessons led to an armament race and a world war.

The bane of stable societies or of stable international systems is the inability to conceive of a mortal challenge. The blind spot of revolutionaries is the belief that the world for which they are striving will combine all the benefits of the new conception with the good points of the overthrown structure. But any upheaval involves costs. The forces unleashed by revolution have their own logic which is not to be deduced from the intentions of their advocates.

So it was with Bismarck. Within five years of coming to power in 1862, he had solved the problem of German unity along the lines of the memoranda he had written during the previous decade. He first induced Austria to separate herself from the secondary German states and to undertake a joint expedition with Prussia against Denmark over the status of Schleswig-Holstein. With Austria isolated from its traditional supporters, Bismarck brought ever increasing pressure on her until in exasperation she declared war. A rapid Prussian victory led to the expulsion of Austria from Germany. Prussia was now free to organize North Germany on a hegemonic basis.

Shortly after taking office, Bismarck had obtained Russian good will by adopting a benevolent attitude during the Polish rebellion of 1862. Napoleon was kept quiet by the lure of gains now in the Rhineland, now in Belgium, now in Luxembourg — prospects that always proved elusive when Napoleon sought to implement them. When Napoleon sought compensation for his miscalculation that Austria would win the Austro-Prussian war, he found himself outmaneuvered. When his mounting frustrations led to the Franco-Prussian war, German unification became a reality at last in 1871.

This united Germany was far from the ideals of those who had urged it for nearly two generations. It was a federation of the historical states and came into being not through the expression of popular will, but through a diplomatic compact among sovereigns.

The very magnitude of Bismarck's achievement mortgaged the future. To be sure, he was as moderate in concluding his wars as he had been ruthless in preparing them. The chief advocate of reason of state had the wisdom to turn his philosophy into a doctrine of self-limitation once Germany had achieved the magnitude and power he considered compatible with the requirements of security. For nearly a generation, Bismarck helped to preserve the peace of Europe by manipulating the commitments and interests of other powers in a masterly fashion.

But the spirits once called forth refused to be banished by a tour de force, however great. The manner in which Germany was unified deprived the international system of flexibility even though it was based on maxims that presupposed the infinite adaptability of the principal actors. For one thing, there were now fewer participants in the international system. The subtle combinations of the secondary German states in the old Confederation had made possible marginal adjustments which were precluded among the weightier components of the modern era.

Moreover, once the resources of Germany became subject to central direction, pressures toward rigid coalitions increased. In trying to deal with its worst nightmare — an alliance between France and Russia — Germany made this alliance inevitable. As German defense policy was geared to coping with a two-front war, it presented an increasing threat to all its neighbors. A Germany strong enough to deal with its two great neighbors jointly would surely be able to defeat them singly. Thus Germany tended to bring on what it feared most. During the period of the German Confederation, joint action was only possible in the face of overwhelming danger. The uncertainty of these arrangements was one of the reasons why Bismarck had insisted on German unification under Prussian leadership. But he paid a price. What had been a remote contingency became at first a nightmare and then a reality.

These tendencies were reinforced because, with the annexation of Alsace-Lorraine by Germany, France disappeared from the list of potential German allies. The irreconcilable hostility of France meant the elimination of the French option, which in the 1850's Bismarck had considered essential. Henceforth French enmity was the "organic fault of our nature" against which Bismarck had warned in the 1850's. This precluded the policy outlined in the "master report" — of remaining aloof until the other powers were committed. With France available as a potential ally to an opponent of Germany, Bismarck had to attempt to forestall isolation by superior adaptability. But only four great powers remained available for Bismarck's subtle combinations, of which one — Great Britain — was tending toward isolation. Obviously the fewer the factors to be manipulated, the greater is the tendency toward rigidity.

To be sure, while Bismarck governed, these dilemmas were obscured by a diplomatic tour de force based on a complicated system of pacts with Germany at their center. But the very complexity of these arrangements doomed them. A system which requires a great man in each generation sets itself an almost insurmountable challenge, if only because a great man tends to stunt the emergence of strong personalities. When the novelty of Bismarck's tactics had worn off and the originality of his conception came to be taken for granted, lesser men strove to operate his system while lacking his sure touch and almost artistic sensitivity. As a result, what had been the manipulation of factors in a fluid situation eventually led to the petrification of the international system which produced World War I.

Bismarck's less imaginative successors failed even when they strove for "calculability" or "reliability." These qualities seemed more easily attainable by rigid commitments than by the delicate, constantly shifting balancing of Bismarck's policy. Thus Germany wound up with the unconditional commitment to the "worm eaten hulk" of Austria which it had been the whole thrust of Bismarck's policy to avoid.

In this manner it became apparent that the requirements of the national interest were highly ambiguous after all. Bismarck could base self-restraint on a philosophy of self-interest. In the hands of others lacking his subtle touch, his methods led to the collapse of the nineteenth-century state system. The nemesis of power is that, except in the hands of a master, reliance on it is more likely to produce a contest at arms than self-restraint.

Domestically, too, the very qualities that had made Bismarck a solitary figure in his lifetime caused his compatriots to misunderstand him when he had become a myth. They remembered the three wars that had achieved their unity. They forgot the patient preparation that had made them possible and the moderation that had secured their fruits. The constitution designed by Bismarck magnified this trend: The Parliament was based on universal suffrage, but had no control over the government; the government was appointed by the Emperor and was removable by him. Such a system encouraged the emergence of courtiers and lobbyists, but not statesmen. Nationalism unleavened by liberalism turned chauvinistic, and liberalism without responsibility grew sterile.

Thus Germany's great modern figure may well have sown the seeds of its twentieth-century tragedies. "No one eats with impunity from the tree of immortality," wrote Bismarck's friend von Roon, the reorganizer of the Prussian army, about him. The meaning of his life was perhaps best expressed by Bismarck himself in a letter to his wife: "That which is imposing here on earth . . . has always something of the quality of the fallen angel who is beautiful but without peace, great in his conceptions and exertions but without success, proud and lonely."

Bismarck and Napoleon III. The meeting between the Chancellor of the North German Confederation and the Emperor of France in September 1870, after the Battle of Sedan, is depicted in this contemporary print. Bismarck seems serene and confident; Napoleon looks grief-stricken by his defeat and capture. (Archiv für Kunst und Geschichte, Berlin)

PART

III Unifier of Germany

Heinrich von Srbik

The Austrian Tragedy

The decline and fall of the Austrian Empire haunted Heinrich von Srbik all his life. Contemplating the tragic destiny of his country, he came to the conclusion that its mission had been to uphold the supranational unity of Central Europe. In a series of important works he portrayed the Habsburg state as the last stronghold of the universalist tradition of the Middle Ages. His greatest book, *Deutsche Einheit: Idee und Wirklichkeit,* deals with the Austro-Prussian conflict in the nineteenth

Source: Heinrich Ritter von Srbik, *Deutsch Einheit — Idee und Wirklichkeit vom Heiligen Reich bis Königgrätz,* vol. IV, pp. 463–469, © 1942 F. Bruckmann KG, Munich. Translated by Theodore S. Hamerow and William W. Beyer. Reprinted by permission of the publisher.

century. In the following selection Srbik analyzes in his involved, turgid prose the consequences of the Hohenzollern victory of 1866.

In that year the forces of the German past were engaged in a struggle with the youthful forces of German growth regarding the form of German national life. This struggle involved the immanent vital laws of the state; it involved the multiformity of the German spirit arising out of the multiformity of the German body politic, engaged in conflict with the youthful German spirit reflecting the civic unity of the national community. The law of all existence is also valid for the vital political form of great peoples and nations conscious of their destiny. The structure of political existence was and is shaped by creative forces which embody principles and determine appropriate political forms and the nature of law. They lead a life of their own consistent with their time. As long as they possess the capacity for inspiring action, their form and law have a higher justification. But then opposing forces arise, pulsating with a more vigorous life, which demand a new political form and a new law, which triumphantly drive the old powers to exhaustion and death. The unifying and relatively eternal element in the evolution of civic and political forms is the great nation, bound by ties of blood and spirit to a unique organic essence, intimately connected with a geographic area, unfolding its potentialities. Out of the interrelationship of independent nations arises the community of peoples which we call humanity, the world, and Europe. The deed acts as a motive force, reinforcing the energies which create a new order among peoples. But not everything which falls victim, which becomes the past is doomed to death as soon as the new form of life becomes reality thanks to its youthful vigor and its conscious, willful deed.

If we regard the course of German history from this point of view, then we can no longer treat with the usual scorn the many centuries of the first German Empire, the half century of the German Confederation, and the former leading role of Austria in Germany. The aged Holy Roman Empire had at one time lived a life of immeasurable greatness. It died not only through external violence, but through the enfeeblement of an idea embracing and unifying the whole, an idea exercising effective power. The German Confederation, which owed its origins to historic tendencies arising out of the past, which was in many respects the spiritual and political if not the legal heir of the empire, had to perish when the form and the law of the past came into irreconcilable conflict with the living law of the present demanding a new order of things. Such also was the fate of the primacy in German affairs of Austria, the old wearer of the imperial crown, who represented on a reduced scale the faded idea of empire, and who predominated in the German Confederation. And such was the fate of the second German Empire, when in the absence of inspiring goals and of a true, profound conception of the nation, its vital inner energies turned to an overemphasis on material gain and to spiritual discord. External and internal causes always joined in the downfall of the old order, while profound needs and great accomplishments always led to a new act of creation. . . .

In this sense we can clearly comprehend the national and world significance of the year 1866. . . . The German people as an organism required by virtue of its inner law of life a new political order which could secure for it life-giving unity at home and a position of political power in the world in keeping with its greatness. The structure of the German Confederation under the primacy of Austria could no longer satisfy this requirement. Both were too greatly encumbered with the heritage of ideas and forms, with the traditions of centuries to be able to create a vigorous new Germany. As long as the sovereignty of the individual German states in diplomatic and military affairs was not willingly or unwillingly surrendered in favor of the sovereignty of a federal government representing the political interests of the nation, as long as the dualism of two great powers divided Germany, a sound solution of the German problem in the foreseeable future was inconceivable. This German dualism in turn endowed the idea of trialism with a certain vitality. The subordination of one power to the other was an impossibility, since neither Prussia nor Austria could accept the leadership of her opponent. The only alternatives were the curtailment of the power of one of the two great states to the point of its absorption into a greater Germany led by its rival, or the exclusion of one of the two great states, in other words, a smaller Germany. The separation of Prussia from the German body politic was something which the purely Prussian outlook of King William could at times consider a necessity. This was never true of Bismarck, however, who acted out of Prussian state interest, but maintained that Prussian and German interests were concurrent. The exclusion of Austria from Germany was something which a particularistic Austrian outlook could accept, but this was never true of a German national will directed toward all of the German people and toward Central Europe. The division split the nation down the middle. Austria at that time could not find a way and purpose capable of solving her own problems of organization, while in the vital German question she also found herself in a state of indecision, caught between the demands of an old, dying order and a maturing new epoch. She clung to a formal legality, yet Bismarck and the Prussian state smashed that legality. They became the great destroyers of the inclusive German Confederation, just as once Prussia had grown great at the expense of the Holy Roman Empire, contributing significantly to its collapse through Frederick the Great. But both of them, the creative political genius and his state, offered non-Austrian Germany something which Austria could not offer: a vital order, the unity of will and action of the majority of the people. Here was their higher historical function in Germany, here was their higher legality vis-à-vis Austria.

This function and legality strengthened them also in dealing with the world of the middle and small states of Germany, the most loyal advocates besides Austria of the associative, federative principle. In honor of the German past let it be said once more that even in the old inclusive outlook of this third Germany there was a great deal of strong German consciousness and genuine love for the entire nation, along with particularism and separatism of various sorts. But the reform from which even many members of the Diet of the Confederation hopefully expected a revival of German power and German spirit was thwarted not only by the opposition of Prussia, but also by the nature of the confederation itself, by the irreconcilable divisions within the third group of states, by the inability to satisfy the vital claim of the nation to a truly new form of existence establishing federal unity and freedom for all of Germany. Yet it was precisely this goal which Bismarck attained by the revolution from above, in opposition to the majority of the German and the Prussian people. The dream which he had dreamed early in 1863, at a time of great strain, became reality. In that dream he is riding up a narrow Alpine path, an abyss on the right, cliffs to the left. And then the horse refuses to go on. It is impossible to turn around or dismount. With the whip which he is holding in his left hand he strikes the smooth wall of the rock and calls on God. The whip begins to extend, and the wall of the rock slides away like scenery on a stage, opening a broad passage with a view of hills and forests like those of Bohemia, revealing Prussian troops and banners.

The architect of the second German Empire never became an advocate of a greater Germany including Austria. But even the "striving for Germany" in the form of a smaller empire was not as yet apparent in his peace negotiations of 1866. He who had approached and solved the German problem always keeping in mind its European context could not as yet consider at Nikolsburg and Prague his second objective, the national unification of Germany under Prussian hegemony without Austria, because of the other Great Powers. Did not France for reasons of "security" demand Bavarian and Hessian territory left of the Rhine, including the fortress of Mainz, Luxemburg, and Limburg? Did not Bismarck need the support of Russia, whose fear of a revolution in Poland grew as soon as the victor incited revolution in the Danubian monarchy, who looked with disfavor on any serious weakening of Austria, on the extensive Prussian annexations, on the dethronement of dynasties? Her tsar hoped for the joint intervention of the neutral Great Powers, urging the convocation of a congress. It was because of the tsar that Bismarck had to spare the south German states and leave Oberhessen to the grand duchy. He spared Saxony in deference to Austria, content to persuade his king to approve the complete annexation of Hanover and Hesse-Kassel which aroused only platonic feelings in England and Russia. His design did not extend beyond what could be safely attained. On August 1, 1866, he wrote to his son Wilhelm: "What we need is north Germany, and that is where we want to expand." In the new organization of Germany he allowed the south German states to remain politically independent side by side with the North German Confederation. But he crossed the boundary of the Main River by means of defensive and offensive alliances. The future might bring "opportunity and luck." A new empire was seen by Bismarck in 1866 as only a desirable possibility, yet that same year also opened the way for its realization.

What died at Königgrätz was not only the old empire which, as has already often been pointed out, had found a continuation of its ideal in the German Confederation; the old Central Europe and the old Europe also died. The famous exclamation of the Papal Secretary of State Cardinal Antonelli, *"Casca il mondo, Casca il mondo,"* expressed the truth. Now that a strong Germany under strong leadership had arisen, even if not as yet in the form of a legally organized political community, the position of France as arbiter and hegemon of the Continent, the result and bulwark of German disunity, was destined to end. It was no longer possible for the neighboring power to divide Germany in two at the most vulnerable point in the west, in the most vital region of the old German Empire. "Germany's misfortune," to use the phrase of Edmund Jörg, was now at an end, the misfortune "that we in Germany support one and a half million soldiers in our budgets, and yet must tremble at every frown of the imperator." With Austria, the empire, and the confederation fell also the remnants of the old universalist, political connection of the German nation to Rome.

With good reason did Pope Pius IX in 1860 insert the name of the emperor of Austria in place of the *Imperator Romanorum* in the liturgical prayer on Good Friday. With good reason did he say at the beginning of the year of decision: "There are only two sovereigns who defend the eternal principles on which thrones rest, Emperor Francis Joseph and I." While the residence city of the Romano-German emperors for long centuries, the capital of the Austrian imperial state, was being threatened by the Prussian army columns, while the Diet of the German Confederation was fleeing as the Prussian regiments marched into the free city on the Main, an English diplomat spoke of the end of the indirect universal rule of Austria which had extended from the Eider to Brindisi, he spoke of the destruction for all time of the Austrian dream of the Holy Roman Empire. Prussia achieved the victory of the national over the universal principle not only in German national life, but for the Italian nation as well. Without Prussia and Bismarck, Italy would not have attained what was essentially the completion of her national unification. The evacuation of the fortresses of the Quadrilateral, the transfer of Venetia to Napoleon and by him to Victor Emmanuel — how could the state vanquished at Custozza and Lissa have won these prizes without Königgrätz? And on July 3, 1866, the temporal rule of the pope over Rome and the *Patrimonium Petri* suffered what was to prove a fatal blow, until the third of the wars of German unification destroyed it completely.

The higher law of life and death decreed that twelve million Germans in Austria should become the victims of the partial unity which was the good fortune of a great majority of the nation. The period of Austria's leadership in the great German commonwealth would not have come to an end in 1866 without Bismarck, but it could not have continued much longer in any event. A great people conscious of its right to life would have sooner or later, peacefully or by force, rejected all artificial political forms as a matter of inner necessity. It would have rejected the primacy of a triumphant Austria in a new confederation including a weakened Prussia and strengthened middle states, a confederation which might represent the proper geographic boundaries, but not the true civic unity of the nation. It would have rejected a division of Germany into a northern confederation under Prussian and a southern confederation under Austrian leadership, for such an arrangement, as Kübeck says, could not have permanently suppressed the yearning of the nation "to build again a whole state out of the two half Germanys." It would have rejected the trialistic fantasies of the passionately patriotic Hermann Orges, who envisioned a "purely German" confederation under the presidency of the emperor of Austria, and then perhaps in the distant future the emergence of a "higher confederation" including both large states. The withdrawal of the German element of Austria from the German body politic was the result of a terrible operation, which by amputating a limb brought new strength and rich development to a sick body. Never again could the old, lax, inclusive system be revived, as Francis Joseph hoped in the first years after Königgrätz.

The historical thought and sentiment of the old advocates of a greater German commonwealth could not comprehend that the bonds which had endured for a millennium were broken. They saw only violence, perfidy, and illegality at work, failing to recognize the profound causes of change. While the political Catholics stood mourning at the grave of their Catholic *grossdeutsch* world and their dream of a Catholic empire, they also felt a genuine, national grief at the loss of their German brothers in Austria. They shared the spirit of Biegeleben's angry sonnets. Königgrätz and its political consequences also produced a sense of deep shock among the liberal protagonists of a *grossdeutsch* state. There is, for example, the gripping poem "Königgrätz" by the Hessian democrat Adam Trabert, in which a German Austrian wounded by a Prussian bullet cries out in anguish: "I lie here deep in clover, slain by my German brethren." Besides burning grief at the separation of German Austria from the nation as a whole, there was in German hearts on both sides of the new frontier bleak pessimism about Austria's future and despair concerning the fate of the separated part of the nation.

Hermann Oncken

Gallic Ambition

In his scholarship Hermann Oncken belonged to the Rankean tradition. He believed that historians must judge calmly and dispassionately, without rancor or patriotic zeal. But in his treatment of French diplomacy during the 1860s, he could not suppress a national pride that was intensified by Germany's humiliation at Versailles in 1919. His study *Napoleon III and the Rhine* was based on thorough research, but there can be no mistaking the villain of the piece. Whether embodied in Louis Napoleon or Raymond Poincaré, Gallic ambition leads inexorably to war.

With soldierly frankness the French military attaché in Berlin, Colonel Stoffel, discussed the true cause of the war at the time of its outbreak. He said that the war was the result of the preponderance of Prussia since 1866 and that this preponderance required France to secure her boundaries. Such security, he felt, she could attain only by acquiring the German territory west of the Rhine, and French possession of the Rhine alone could guarantee the peace between the two nations. These utterances are in agreement with the facts as we have revealed them according to the documents, except that the documents go even further and show that already prior to the war of 1866 Napoleon had a Rhine policy and by an unsuccess-

Source: From *Napoleon III and the Rhine* by Hermann Oncken, pp. 183–194. Copyright 1928 by Alfred A. Knopf, Inc. Reprinted by permission of the publisher.

ful intrigue had himself helped to establish the order which later he believed he could subvert only by conquering the Rhine. This is corroborated by the fact that as late as August 6, the day of the battle of Wörth, Prince Metternich, who had a deeper insight than anyone else into the Napoleonic policies of 1863–1870, spoke outright of the Rhine as the chief war aim. This fact, usually kept dark in France nowadays, was emphasized on September 18, 1919, by the French socialist J. Longuet in a parliamentary address, when he said that it should not be forgotten that the yearning for the left bank of the Rhine was responsible for the war of 1870.

In July 1870, to be sure, French diplomacy had to speak a quite different language abroad. The louder the rabble in Paris clamored for the Rhine, the more zealously did France try to make the outside world believe that she was waging no war of aggression. Although there was little enough serious hope of winning over the south German states, the French government, in all declarations made prior to the final decision of south Germany, made a particular point of stating that it did not intend to take an inch of German soil and wished merely to check the further growth of Prussia. Gramont even went so far as expressly to disavow to the Bavarian minister the demands for the Rhine voiced by the Paris press and was careful to have this noble renunciation loudly proclaimed especially in the Viennese press, so that public sentiment in German Austria might not be estranged but might be prepared for a war on the side of France.

But did these formal declarations, which culminated in Napoleon's war manifesto of July 23, contain the whole truth, or did they admit of evasion and doubtful interpretation? . . . Denmark was to receive as the minimum price of her cooperation all of Schleswig — in other words territory of distinctly German stamp which had been hotly contested for a generation. And what the French were prepared to offer Austria in the event of cooperation, is clear from the negotiations carried on ever since 1866. There can be no doubt that in case of victory not only Silesia would have changed hands; it is more than likely that the old Austrian craving for Bavarian territory would have cropped up again too. And what of the specifically French war objectives?

While publicly stressing nonannexation, Paris found it necessary to resort once more to the substitute for pure annexation which it had for years advocated as a solution compatible with German self-respect and national consciousness, and sugared with so many secret hopes. The autonomous Rhineland state appears once more as a French war aim in the decisive hour. At any rate the French minister in Stuttgart allowed this rather obscure remark to escape him:

> *According to the plans made in Paris in the last few years it is the French aim, in case of victory, to establish a state of about five million inhabitants along the Rhine, perhaps for the King of Hanover.*

Gramont too spoke to the Bavarian minister of a restoration and enlargement of Hanover in order to destroy the Prussian preponderance. Although he considered it more expedient not to mention the Rhineland state expressly, he revealed his intention in another way by hinting at the "annulment" of Baden as a Prussian subsidiary. It will be remembered that it was Gramont too who as early as April 1867, had offered the Austrians south Germany as far as the Black Forest and had shown a special French interest only for Baden. These few points will suffice to disclose the extent of French "renunciation" with respect to German soil. In reverting to the old idea of a neutral state along the Rhine, as a policy which ought to prove acceptable to Europe, France realized of course that in case the treaty of peace were really dictated in Berlin, this modest policy, which was always considered a minimum requirement, would not have to stand.

But the French revealed not only individual phases of their war program. At one point they developed the program in its entirety, though in a discreet form. We refer to the declaration which Gramont early in August was indiscreet enough to make to the Russian chargé in official form, describing it expressly as containing the minimum demands of France. This list includes annexation pure and simple. In demanding the cession of the Saar basin Gramont clearly violated the solemn promise not to claim even a bit of German territory. As for the boundaries in 1814, which ever since 1860 were regarded as the most modest satisfaction of French needs, French diplomacy was accustomed to regard them as resting on an old legal title. But the sum total of the German territorial modifications, which France communicated without hesitation to this friend of Prussia, is even more impressive. It included the reduction of Prussia to the boundaries of 1866 and restoration of the dispossessed; enlargement of the middle states at the expense of ancient Prussian territory, and "constitution of state groups in Germany which would permanently break the Prussian supremacy." This formula expresses the well-known aim of dividing Germany into as many equally large states as possible, the aim which had been made the basis of the Franco-Austrian negotiations of 1869. No evidence is necessary to prove that in this grouping the neutralized Rhineland state with a generous allotment of territory was to play an important part and would in a sense have symbolized the federalistic dismemberment of Germany.

In one respect the war aims communicated by Gramont to the Russians contain a surprise — a feature which at the same time explains the reason why they were communicated at all. At the end the French minister asked the Russian government the official question what it planned to do if the French army should reach Berlin and offer Danzig to Russia in return for her neutrality. This free disposition of German territory, which thus revealed designs even against the eastern German frontier, is the last official expression of the French war aims, made only a short time before the first skirmish at Weissenburg.

In the light of all these French plans, which, be it noted, must be regarded as minimum demands, it becomes clear how perfidious was the war manifesto wherein Napoleon announced to the world his desire that "the peoples forming the great Germanic nation shall be free to control their own destinies." The announcement of the manifesto that it was planned to establish an order "guaranteeing our security for the future" is of the same ilk. The persistent use of such phrases for centuries did not serve to make them more plausible. The picture of the Germany of the Peace of Westphalia, exposed on every side to invasion and disruption, and with all internal bonds loosened to a degree of utter defenselessness — this was the historical ideal of the past which dominated the plans of the present. It was "the great idea" of the French policy, according to Thiers, to disorganize the German state to such an extent that security and aggrandizement would fall to the happy lot of its French neighbor.

Against this menace, which had barely been avoided in 1866, the Germans had to defend their unity and independence in 1870.

In this latter year it was the last echo of those Napoleonic speculations which we discovered as being the secret forces impelling the empire for the seven years between 1863 and 1870. But during a more recent period of seven years, from 1919 to 1926, we have learned by experience that the rhythm of French history is still guided by its initial principle, that this nation, impelled by the force of tradition, can not resist the evil temptations which surround it.

The policy of Napoleon and the French, which opposed Germany's national right of self-determination, led to the war of 1870. Was it justifiable for this policy to defend its fateful course of action before the bars of history by pleading the "security" of France? Is such justification admissible? We have seen how after 1866 the motive of security gradually met the requirements of the new situation and supplanted that of aggrandizement. But it was only a new name for an old concept — the concept of national frontiers, Romano-Gallic reminiscences, pseudo-historical feudal rights and other attempts to clothe gross reality in a palliating mantle of ideas. Two generations earlier the attainment of the national frontiers had been looked upon in France as a sacred tradition. "It is the doctrine of the scholar," said Sorel, "the creed of the poet, the ambition of the popular leader, of the kings, the ministers, the generals, the political meetings, and the committees; it is a question of interests for the economist, a reason of state for the politician, a national dream." All these spheres of life forthwith seized upon the motive of security, and thus revived once more a great historical tradition. This tradition, though it spoke in terms of defense, had in reality an offensive purpose, for it strove to disturb or diminish the national unity of its neighbor. It was animated by the theory that its own security, unity and peace could be maintained only if that neighbor were doomed to insecurity, disunity and unrest, and in advocating this theory it violated the unwritten law of morality which guides the life of nations and sets bounds to the egoism of national interests.

The struggles of the past are of interest for the historical consciousness of the European nations only when their motives and impulses live on in the present as a determining factor. The line which runs from Louis XIV directly to Napoleon III becomes in the end a prime cause for the war of 1870–1871. This fact was clear to the generation which fought that war. To the numerous judgments of other nations we may add the opinion of the American minister Bancroft, the renowned historian. On October 12, 1870, he spoke the following confidential words in the Berlin foreign office:

> *The leading statesmen as well as public opinion in America regard the present war essentially as an act of self-defence on Germany's part, and the outstanding task is to insure Germany permanently, by a better system of frontiers, against new wars of aggression on the part of her western neighbors, of which the past three centuries have brought so large a number.*

The real facts began to be obscured when, with the formation of the great coalition against Germany, the French conception was adopted by the political allies of France. And since the World War the question of the causes of the war of 1870 was, for political reasons, still more obscured and supplanted by a legend which described the latter as merely a step preliminary to the former. The causes of both wars were merged in one large question of guilt, so presented that those who, in France or in countries intellectually dependent upon her, believed in the exclusive or principal responsibility of Germany for the World War, were led to believe also the legend that France was attacked by Germany in 1870. But while the French undertook to reconstruct a fictitious past and to invent the story of the French lamb and the German wolf, it happened that the newly aroused spirit of their historical Rhineland policy, endowed with a new halo and unhampered by diplomatic considerations, has in recent years since the World War given ever more damaging testimony of them. What we have detected as the secret motive power of French politics ever since 1815 and as the Napoleonic ambition which from 1863 on led to the catastrophe, now became more irresistible than ever before. Almost all parties, with a few exceptions, now endorsed the claim for the Rhine, and all along the line scholarship, animated by a spirit which Albert Sorel had once castigated, argued the historical right of that claim, enlisting self-interest and sentiment in the service of a consistent endeavor, which varied but in the details of method and advocated now annexation pure and simple and now some form of Rhineland state, either neutral or at least independent of Prussia and in any case exposed to penetration. This device, of course, had always been the first step toward conquest, and during the dark days of confusion after 1919 it found, even in Germany, sympathetic fools and treacherous advocates who did not realize whose interests would be served by any change in the established order along the Rhine.

If the causes of the war of 1870 are to be linked and associated with those of the World War, well and good. History justifies such a procedure, but not in the sense in which the enemies of Germany, who would make her alone responsible for the World War, interpret it. The French national tradition which drove Napoleon III into the war and brought about the fateful clash between the historical Rhineland policy of the French and the right of self-determination of the German people is the cradle of that spirit of revenge which played so important a part in bringing about the international tension leading to the World War. The same spirit which inspired the secret forces of the French national soul has imposed upon it a large measure of guilt before the bars of mankind. Inasmuch as this spirit prevents a permanent reconciliation of the two nations after the catastrophe, it has remained to this day the most serious obstruction to all hopes for future pacific intercourse among the nations of Europe.

Émile Ollivier

The Eternal Boche

The last fifty years of Émile Ollivier's life were one long anticlimax. After winning an early reputation as a brilliant lawyer, he had plunged into the turbulent politics of the Second Empire. His forceful agitation in favor of parliamentary rule led to his appointment as prime minister early in 1870. It was an unfortunate time to be in power in Paris. Seven months later he was forced to resign in the midst of defeat during the Franco-Prussian War. Thereafter there was nothing for him to do but meditate on the glories of the past and seek vicarious vengeance against Bismarck in his voluminous memoirs. His death in 1913 came on the eve of another war, which was to reverse the verdict of Sedan.

Source: From Émile Ollivier, *The Franco-Prussian War and Its Hidden Causes* (Boston: Little, Brown and Company, 1912), pp. 5–9, 400–404.

The first cause of the war of 1870 is to be found in the year 1866. It was in that year, to be marked forever with black, it was in that year of blindness when one error was redeemed only by a more grievous error, and when the infirmities of the government were made mortal by the bitterness of the opposition; it was in that accursed year that was born the supreme peril of France and of the empire. If the year 1870 is the terrible year, 1866 is the fatal year. The Romans according to Cicero, considered the battle of the Allia more disastrous than the taking of Rome because that last misfortune was the result of the first.

Everybody, in all Europe as well as in France, is in accord touching the importance of the fateful year, and this historic truth is not contested. But everywhere the error committed by Napoleon III is mistakenly characterized. It was his chimerical loyalty to the principle of nationalities, people say, which led him to allow Prussia to constitute a great power that was a menace to ourselves. Say just the contrary, and you will be in right. It was his disloyalty to the principle of nationalities that was the source of all of Napoleon III's misfortunes and our own.

People would not deny it if they had a better comprehension of this theory of nationalities, which everybody talks about without understanding it, or understanding it all awry. The theory of nationalities may be reduced to a few maxims of luminous simplicity:

> *Every freely constituted nation forms a sovereign, intangible organism, however weak, which cannot be placed under foreign domination without its consent, or be kept there against its will. It does not recognize conquest as a legitimate means of acquisition. Only the will of the people has the power lawfully to create, to transform, to diminish, or to increase kingdoms.*
>
> *Whence it follows: first, that no nation has the right to meddle in the affairs of another, to object to its international arrangements, to prevent it from separating from a state to which it was united by force, or from annexing itself to another to which it is drawn by its sympathies or its interests. Furthermore, Europe, assembled in congress or conference, is not possessed of a collective right of its own, which is denied to each nation separately, on the pretext of preventing any nation from disturbing, at its pleasure, the general system to which it belongs.*

The underlying principle of the theory of nationalities is easily distinguishable from others with which it is too often confused — that of great agglomerations, of natural boundaries, and of race. The will of the people concerned may, if it seems fitting, constitute great agglomerations, but it may constitute small ones as well. It does not recognize natural frontiers. The real frontiers are those established by the will of the people; the others are the walls of a prison, which one has always the right to tear down. Woe to the country that drags a province in its train like a millstone about its neck; woe to that one whose people do not bask in its sunshine with free and joyful hearts. To create moral unity is more essential than to satisfy the strategic demands of a mountain-chain or a stream.

Nor does the theory of nationalities recognize a pretended right of race, manifested by a common language or by historic tradition, by virtue of which all the nations born of a common stock and speaking the same language must needs, whether they will or no, and without being consulted, be united in a single state. The idea of race is a barbarous, exclusive, retrograde idea, and has nothing in common with the broad, sacred, civilizing idea of fatherland. Race has limits which cannot be overstepped; fatherland has none; it may expand and develop unceasingly; it might become all mankind, as under the Roman Empire. On our European continent races long since became blended in fatherlands, and it would be impossible to undo the mysterious process from which have flowed the beautiful products of that blending.

There is an ineffable sweetness in the word *fatherland*, just because it expresses, not a preordained aggregation, but a free, loving creation, wherein millions of human beings have placed their hearts for centuries past.

The will of the peoples, then, is the one dominant, sovereign, absolute principle, whence the modern law of nations in its entirety should flow by a series of logical deductions, as from an inexhaustible spring. It is the principle of liberty substituted in international relations for geographical and historical inevitableness.

Of course the principle of nationality does not do away with all wars. There remain the wars waged for honor, for religion, for the diversion of despots; but it eliminates the most common and most dangerous sort—those of conquest; and it tends toward the progressive abolition of other wars, by virtue of the civilizing principle which is its inspiration. It should be cultivated everywhere with respect, and propagated by men of progress and liberty. In France it should be a national dogma, since it is our incontestable right to reconquer our dear Alsace, brutally wrested from us by conquest, and annexed to the foreigner without her consent.

Were the events that occurred in Germany in 1866 the logical outcome of the principle of nationalities? Was it by virtue of that principle as we have defined it, that Prussia annexed the Danish Duchies, the free towns, Frankfurt, Hesse-Darmstadt, and Hanover, although it was the declared desire of the peoples thereof to retain their autonomy? No, it was by virtue of a denial of that principle that those annexations were carried out. Bismarck, who was not fond of hypocritical euphemisms of speech, said in so many words, "It was by right of conquest." The year 1866, therefore, was not the triumph of the principle of nationality, but its defeat, and the victorious resurrection of the principle of conquest. The real error of Napoleon III consisted, not in forwarding that civilizing principle, which had already raised him so high, but in becoming the compliant tool, in the hope of a reward, of those who were rending it with their swords.

He was at liberty not to oppose by force the conquest of Prussia, if he did not consider that the interest of France demanded it; but he should have seconded the efforts which others (Russia, for example) were making to arrest them, and, in any event, should not have approved, much less have encouraged them, and, less still, have demanded a reward for that encouragement. But that is what he did: he gave Prussia his formal assent, refused to second Russia in suggesting the assembling of a congress, and solicited, as a reward, first the left bank of the Rhine, then Belgium, and finally Luxembourg.

Prussia welcomed his adhesion with sarcastic cordiality, and refused with insolent ingratitude the wage, even when it was reduced to the minimum. She did more: she snapped her fingers at the man to whose kindly neutrality she was indebted for not being crushed on the battlefield, and she instantly disregarded the promise she had made at Prague to arrest her predominance at the Main: she passed that boundary, in a military sense, by means of treaties of alliance, and thus constituted the military unity of Germany — the only form of unity which was dangerous to us. . . .

The cause of the conflict between Germany and France was only one of those "artificial fatalities," born of the false conceptions or unhealthy ambitions of statesmen, which with lapse of time become worn out, transformed, and often extinguished. If France had but resolutely made up her mind not to meddle in the affairs of Germany, not to regard German unity as a menace or as a lessening of her own importance, it would have seemed perfectly natural to her that a nation so powerful in every way — in intelligence, imagination, poetry, science, and arms — should shape herself as she chose, with full liberty of spontaneous action.

On the other hand, if the German professors, content with the memories of 1814 and of Waterloo, could but have made up their minds to forget the Palatinate and Jena, on the instant this alleged fatality of war would have vanished, and the only relation between the two nations, established by mutual consent, would have been one of friendly cooperation in the common task of spreading light and of emancipation from real fatalities. That was the hope to which I devoted my conduct in international matters, and which, as minister, I would have brought to fruition had my power endured.

But there was a man to whom it was important that that artificial fatality should exist and should end in war. It was that powerful genius, who, not choosing to abandon to time the glory of achieving slowly the work of unity, whose hour of triumph was inevitable, determined to hasten the evolution, to force upon the present what the future would have accomplished freely, and to retain for himself alone the glory which his successors would otherwise have shared. With him out of the way, war between France and Germany would have ceased to be predestined, and the son of Napoleon III would have escaped it as well as his father.

Napoleon III wanted peace, but with a vacillating will; Bismarck wanted war, with an inflexible will: the inflexible will overcame the vacillating will. A fresh proof, as that profound thinker Gustave Le Bon so forcibly says, that "the faith that raises mountains is named the will. It is the true creator of things."

So that it is a pitiful thing to read these labored dissertations of our trumpery historians, searching for what they call responsibilities, and struggling to incriminate, some the statesmen of the opposition, others those of the government. Unquestionably the opposition were so short-sighted as to keep alive an irritable agitation in men's minds; unquestionably the emperor should not have re-opened, by a fruitless demand of guaranties, a question already closed by a triumphant solution. But neither the declamations of the opposition, nor the mistake of Napoleon III, were the decisive cause of the war. No Frenchman was responsible for it. The only man who will have the glory or the shame of it, whichever posterity may adjudge it to be, is the man of iron, whose indomitable and heroic will controlled events and made them serve his ambition.

Demosthenes said to the Athenians: "Let an orator rise and say to you: 'It is Diopithus who causes all your ills; it is Chares, or Aristophon,' or any other that it pleases him to name, and instantly you applaud and exclaim loudly, 'Oh! how truly he speaks!' But let a plain-spoken man say to you: 'O Athenians! the sole author of your ills is Philip' — that truth angers you; it is even as an arrow that wounds you." And I say to our Athenians: "The war was let loose upon us neither by Diopithus, nor by Chares, nor by Aristophon, but by Philip, and in 1870 Philip's name was Bismarck."

One of Bismarck's panegyrists, Johannes Scherr, has described most excellently the character that should be attributed to the creator of German unity.

After producing so many giants of thought, Germany was destined to produce, at last, a hero of deeds. In the age of the Reformation, and later, we had had an abundance of idealists, but not a politician. We lacked the practical genius, the genius unhampered by schedules. Yes, just that, in very truth! For reflecting and experienced men must needs leave where it deserves to be, that is to say, in the child's primer, the worn-out commonplace which declares that "the most honest politician is the best." There has never been such a thing as an honest politician, in the ordinary sense of the phrase, and there ought never to be. The creative statesman should perform his allotted task without taking pains to find out whether his adversaries consider it "dishonest," or whether it is unpleasant or harmful to them. It is not the ethereal arguments of a subjective idealism, but stern realities, super-prosaic material interests, as well as commonplace and exalted passions, which in combination make the science of statecraft.

Thus would Bismarck have liked to be praised — in such terms it is fitting to speak of that extraordinary man, the craftiest of foxes, the boldest of lions, who had the art of fascinating and of terrifying, of making of truth itself an instrument of falsehood; to whom gratitude, forgiveness of injuries, and respect for the vanquished were as entirely unknown as all other noble sentiments save that of devotion to his country's ambition; who deemed legitimate everything that contributes to success and who, by his contempt for the importunities of morality, dazzled the imagination of mankind.

After the affair of the Duchies, as our ambassador, Talleyrand, was seeking some roundabout phrase by which to express a certain degree of disapproval, "Don't put yourself out," said Bismarck, "nobody but my King thinks that I acted honorably."

Aesthetically, I like him thus. So long as he denies the evidence, plays the virtuous, the guileless man, outdoes himself in tartufferie, he lowers himself to the point of making himself contemptible. As soon as he reveals his true self and boasts of his audacious knaveries which raised his Germany, until then divided and impotent, to the first rank among the nations, then he is as great as Satan — a Satan beautiful to look upon. Bismarck hatching in the dark the Hohenzollern candidacy, without a suspicion that war will inevitably be the result, would be a zany to be hooted at; Bismarck devising that same plot because it is the sole means of causing the outbreak of the war which he must have in order to achieve the unity of his fatherland, is a mighty statesman, of sinister but impressive grandeur. He will not thereby have opened for himself the gates of any Paradise; he will have won forever one of the most exalted places in the German Pantheon of terrestrial apotheoses.

Hans Rothfels

A Historic Necessity

No one has defended Bismarck with greater perception and understanding than Hans Rothfels. A lifelong opponent of totalitarianism in all its varieties, he left Germany for America during the Third Reich. But for him a world of difference separated the ideals of the Iron Chan-

Source: Hans Rothfels, "Problems of a Bismarck Biography," *Review of Politics*, 4 (1947), pp. 375–380. Reprinted with permission from Review of Politics.

cellor and those of National Socialism. As for the unification of Germany, there was no alternative to the policy of blood and iron. Bismarckian diplomacy admittedly relied on power, but it was power used with moderation and restraint. In his article "Problems of a Bismarck Biography" Rothfels took issue with Erich Eyck's interpretation of the founder of the German Empire.

This brings the discussion back to Mr. Eyck's underlying assumption that the German national unity which he himself finds natural, would have been attainable by other and less forceful means than those of Bismarck. This is a hypothesis which, of course, can neither be proved nor repudiated. It can be said, however, and in view of many legends it seems a matter of fairness to do so today, that there was little "western" sympathy with the attempt at founding a "good" German Reich, that is, one on the liberal-democratic basis of 1848. While Disraeli spoke of "the 50 mad professors at Frankfurt," Palmerston felt alarmed by the development of a *"nation inconnue jusqu'ici au Foreign Office."* And Thiers later confessed that if he could have had his way in 1848 he would have extended the French frontiers to the Rhine and taken "the keys of Germany" into hand. When it eventually came to the half-liberal policy of union in 1850 it ended with a deadlock enforced by a Russo-Austrian ultimatum. Even Radowitz's very moderate aims would have to be carried out by arms. Nor was the diplomatic record of the new era in Prussia altogether promising. When the liberal policy of moral conquest was at its height in 1860, the *London Times* had this to say:

> Prussia is always leaning on somebody, always getting somebody to help her, never willing to help herself; always ready to deliberate, never to decide; present in congresses, but absent in battles; speaking and writing, never for or against, but only on, the question; ready to supply any amount of ideals or sentiments, but shy of anything that savors of the real or the actual. She has a large army, but notoriously one in no condition for fighting. She is profuse in circulars and notes, but has generally a little to say for both sides. No one counts on her as a friend, no one dreads her as an enemy. How she became a Great Power history tells us, why she remains so nobody can tell. . . . Prussia

> *unaided could not keep the Rhine or the Vistula for a month from her ambitious neighbors.*

Mr. Eyck has a rather optimistic view of these ambitious neighbors, in particular of the French tradition of advancing to the east, a view which was shared neither by the German socialists circa 1860 nor by the lauded Konstantin Frantz for that matter. It seems worthy of mentioning that the federalist thinker started from the very assumption of a double threat to *Mitteleuropa*. He therefore advocated a universal system in the center of the continent with a voluntary union of the historic states as its nucleus, a loose German and non-German federation, which Holland, Sweden, Denmark might join and England might protect. Such a system would guarantee peace by turning Russia's and France's ambitions to Asia and North Africa respectively. One may pay high tribute to this idealistic scheme and yet seriously doubt its chance of overcoming particularism by persuasion or achieving a British willingness to enter upon Central European commitments and to sympathize with the economic perspectives of a great federative bloc (united by mutual preferences!). It is only in an entirely different situation, against the background of a post-Bismarckian development and with foreign powers ruling over Central Europe, that the federalist concept or rather that of a "Central European Switzerland" has gained a new meaning.

It would appear then that the consolidation of the weak center of Europe presupposed other means than those suggested by Frantz and that the nucleus had to be created by diplomatic action rather than by a plea for sympathy or a moral appeal. Whether war was absolutely necessary may be doubted and certainly can not be demonstrated. But it is definitely wrong to say that only the forceful foundation of the Reich of 1871 produced the *cauchemar des coalitions* as a sort of self-inflicted punishment. The conviction of a double threat was not of Bismarck's making. It had been widespread among the liberals of Germany around 1860 in the same sense as it was shared by Frantz. And it was the basis of Bismarck's diplomacy before 1870 just as much as afterwards it was simply a Central European fact. Only by a new distribution of power and a new security, in Bismarck's view, could the aim be reached (which he had in common with Frantz), of turning Russia's and France's ambitions "to Asia and North Africa respectively."

This criticism of some federalist illusions, however, should not prevent us from seeing that the pre- or supra-national and anticentralistic elements in the structure of Bismarck's Reich came nearer to a basic federalism than is ordinarily realized. On this point Mr. Eyck's book falls particularly short of the mark. The fact that Bismarck stressed the institutional links between the old German Confederation and the new Reich, that he checked the Reichstag and its universal suffrage by the "anonymous-phalanx" of the federative council, that he kept the competence of the central organs within very narrow limits, that he resisted successfully a responsible Reichsministry — all this was, in the author's view, mere tactics and only meant to concentrate the real power in Prussia and, in the last analysis, in Bismarck's hands. There is truth in this interpretation, not a new one for that matter, but it is by far not the full truth or the most substantial part of it. Again all evidences are omitted which refer to some of the underlying principles. It is certainly not uninteresting and beside the point to recall today such principles as Bismarck expressed in the Reichstag (April 16, 1869): " . . . In Germanic states one should not ask . . . what can be in common, how far can the great mouth of the commonwealth swallow the apple (*hineinbeissen in den Apfel*) — but rather one should ask: what must be absolutely in common." It seems safe to say that Bismarck, quite apart from other elements of his thought, was Junker enough to be antitotalitarian in principle. More consideration should also be given to his plans to supplement the Reichstag by *staendische* organizations. Particularly in connection with the plan for compulsory insurance against accidents, he thought of a network of professional associations to be spread over the country. This again implies antiparliamentary tactics but also an insight into the dangerous process of social atomization. While in all this there was a federalist aspect domestically, the noncentralistic setup of the Reich had a broader meaning as a pattern of transition to other federative forms beyond the frontiers: Germany with her composite character might indicate, as Bismarck pointed out, a method by the use of which "Austria could reach a reconciliation of the political and material interests which exist between the eastern frontiers of the Russians and the Bay of Cattaro."

These potentialities are often overlooked. They are certainly not seen by Mr. Eyck and he seems to be completely and rather naively unaware of the nationalist implications of a unitary and democratic German Reich in Central Europe or of Bruck's "Greater Germany." In contrast Bismarck's national state was no "nation state" proper; it included non-Germans (about 10 percent) and it did not include and ought not to have included all Germans. Jokingly Bismarck once said that, if the nine million contiguous Germans in Austria ever would try to join the Reich, he would wage war against them. In more serious words he admonished them, that instead of harking back, they should take the lead in evolving a multi-national combine in the southeast. The same restraint he observed towards the Germans in Russia, and he did so not only for diplomatic or opportunistic reasons. His so-called *étatisme* may have been a major limitation in some aspects of domestic policy; but what was opposition to democracy was at the same time opposition to nationalism. What was an attempt at checking social atomism was paralleled by a check on the trend towards a national atomism which would disintegrate Central Europe and end in a war of races. That is why Bismarck opposed Pan-Germanism no less than Pan-Slavism.

In this negative attitude — or rather in this conservative restraint — there was implied some positive appraisal of variety and multinational forms of life. There was at least much more of it than liberal and federalist critics usually realize. The crown prince may have been thunderstruck when Bismarck, in 1870, admonished him to have his son learn the Polish language or when he added that all the Prussian rulers down to Frederick the Great had known it — and that he knew it himself. To the liberal biographer these remarks do not seem to have made any more sense than they probably made to the crown prince. Incidentally, Mr. Eyck does not speak of the anti-Polish settlement law of 1886 (*Ansiedlungsgesetz*) which ranks so high on the list of Prussian *hakatism*. As a matter of fact the settlement of German peasants in the eastern provinces was urged by the national liberals. Bismarck yielded to them but professed no sympathy with uprooting the Polish peasants or depriving them of their language. In his old age he spoke of the intermingling of peoples in the east as "riches willed by God." Whatever the shortcomings of this Polish policy he was certainly as remote from racialism and biologism as anyone could be. . . .

But the writer does not want this article to end on a note of professional controversy. There is more at stake than that. We may criticize Bismarck for many good reasons, for paving the way to some fatal trends of our days, but while doing so we cannot very well overlook the fundamental fact that Hitler, in almost every re-spect, did precisely what the founder of the Reich had refused to do. Many of those who were under the heel or outside Germany, had an appreciation of this fact. And thus the word of the Danish historian may be taken up once more as a summary which draws the essential frontier line: Bismarck certainly "belonged to our world," that is, to the anti-Hitlerian world. That this was not generally real-ized is in part the fault of Germans and German historians them-selves. But it may be called a kind of saving grace that a revival of genuine Bismarckian thought (as different from the old Bismarck orthodoxy) was one of the forces which went into the making of the German resistance against Hitler. Specifically "Prussian" elements as far as they remained alive after the landslide of 1933 were also in the anti-Nazi camp. To state this is no longer a matter of any practi-cal importance since these forces have been radically eliminated, but it seems to be a matter of historical justice.

The Berlin Congress. The meeting in Berlin in the summer of 1878 to deal with the Near Eastern question was the most brilliant assembly of European diplomats between the Congress of Vienna in 1814–1815 and the Paris Peace Conference in 1919. In this painting Bismarck stands in the center, shaking hands with Count Peter Shuvalov, one of the Russian delegates, while Foreign Minister Julius Andrassy of Austria-Hungary looks on. (Bildarchiv Preußischer Kulturbesitz, Berlin/Painting by Anton von Werner, 1881)

Arbiter of Europe

Erich Brandenburg

Pax Teutonica

The scholarly career of Erich Brandenburg began in the days of the German Empire and ended after World War II amid the ruins of Hitler's Reich. His reputation rested on several important works dealing with the modern period of history, works characterized by a sober, businesslike, straightforward approach to learning. The writing was solid rather than exciting; at times it could be ponderous. But there was no denying the substantial, thorough quality of his work. Under the Weimar Republic he published a major study of the diplomacy of the period

Source: Erich Brandenburg, *From Bismarck to the World War: A History of German Policy 1870–1914* by Erich Brandenburg translated by Annie Elizabeth Adams. Copyright © 1927, reprinted by permission of Oxford University Press, London.

1871 to 1914, contending that Bismarck's policy during his chancellorship was essentially moderate and peaceful.

The supreme object of Germany's policy, which was controlled by Bismarck until 1890 in spite of various *contretemps*, was the maintenance of European peace. It was not merely stressed in the speeches and manifestoes of our leading men; it was the governing motive in the whole disposition of our policy and in the particular decisions which had to be taken. Knowledge of this has become the common property of historians since the German archives bearing on the Bismarck period have been thrown open for research, no matter what views may be held as to the great chancellor's political conduct or even as to his intentions in particular instances. Our great statesman was of the opinion that we had everything we really needed and that war, even a victorious war, did not offer an actual gain. On the north and the west our territory had actually reached and occasionally even exceeded the limits of our nationality. No thoughtful German has ever wanted to add German Switzerland or Holland to our empire. To bring the German provinces of Austria once more into our national state has seemed to many a desirable aim, and to not a few simply a matter of duty. Nevertheless it was in Catholic southern Germany that these aspirations flourished rather than in the Protestant north which had taken the leading part in the new empire. Bismarck always maintained that the inclusion of the Catholic German Austrians would strengthen the centrifugal forces within the empire; but on the other hand he considered the collapse of Austria a national danger, as the majority of the non-German territories were inhabited by a Slav population who would naturally turn to Russia if the Hapsburg monarchy were dissolved. Such an accession to Russia's power seemed to him ominous both for Germany and for Europe. Hence the maintenance of Austria-Hungary's position as a Great Power became one of the cornerstones of his policy; and so long as he was at the helm and his influence persisted, all thoughts of increase of territory in the southeast were barred. As a matter of fact in the northeast we had already more foreign elements in our empire than was comfortable. To increase the percentage of Polish inhabitants hostile to us would have been a huge blunder. Bismarck never believed that the Baltic provinces, the ruling classes in which were German both by descent and culture, could ever again be drawn into our empire. Geographically these provinces lay too much outside our territory. The majority of their inhabitants were of a different race and were not friendly to us, while even the nobility were much too sympathetic towards Russia — where they played a big part and received special consideration — to wish for union with Germany.

These facts and considerations led Bismarck to the conclusion that we had nothing to gain even from a victorious war in Europe. Besides, our newly-created empire was, so to speak, still in process of formation; time alone would test the new arrangements and prove their worth; sharp differences in religious and social matters constituted a serious menace to us; and, finally, our budding prosperity urgently required peace. Maintenance of existing conditions and of peace had to be the cardinal point of German policy. Bismarck recognized this and acted upon it. In his *Thoughts and Recollections* he declares that his aim was to earn the confidence of lesser and greater powers by a peaceful, just, honest and conciliatory policy. It almost sounds like a belated palliation of his essentially Machiavellian statesmanship. Yet the further we carry our researches, the clearer is the evidence that he was only putting into words the fundamental principle of his actions.

Such being the general position of affairs at that time, what was there to disturb the peace of Europe? There were two centers of constant unrest, two territories whose temporary status was not generally recognized as the foundation of future troubles — Alsace-Lorraine and the Balkans.

At the Peace of Frankfurt, France had been compelled to renounce Alsace-Lorraine. It had been a bitter mortification to her to part with land that for well-nigh two centuries had formed an integral part of her national territory. She overlooked the fact that she had previously conquered by force these provinces from Germany. The demand for their restoration was regarded as an injustice to France and to the territory itself, whose inhabitants were not consulted. Thenceforward the great majority of the French nation regarded it as a matter of course that by some means or other this injustice should be redressed. The loss of the Saar territory in the second Treaty of Paris in 1815 had not been forgotten. Even in

1866, Napoleon III had made an attempt to recover it. Of course the explanation of the French attitude towards Germany's injustice was to be found not only in the loss of territory, but also in the supersession of her dominating position in Europe: after the Prussian victories of 1866 the cry for revenge made itself heard. Anger at military defeat accentuated it. The emergence of a new military German Empire, economically superior, betokened the end of the French hegemony and wounded French pride in its most sensitive spot. Alsace-Lorraine was the outward and visible symbol of the overthrow France had suffered.

French statesmen thoroughly understood that nothing could be done in the immediate future towards realizing these hopes of revenge. France's wounds must be healed, her internal affairs reorganized, her military strength brought up to a far different standard, before she could think of a new war. Well they knew that even later on a struggle of that kind could scarcely be waged single-handed with any prospect of success. Germany was steadily increasing in population and industrial wealth. The population of France was not increasing, her ancient wealth was virtually stationary, while in actual industrial enterprise there was no comparison with Germany. Hence the need of finding allies, and of exploiting every development in the general political situation unfavorable to Germany. France's leading men were firmly convinced that her hour would come when Germany became involved in a war with a third power. German policy had therefore to reckon that in any serious conflict with another power, France would be against her. Therein lay the significance of the Alsace-Lorraine problem in European politics. It was not in itself an acute danger, but it was a latent and persistent threat to peace, because it was evident that in every conceivable situation it would determine France's attitude and would be an unseen factor influencing the grouping of the powers. There were certainly men and tendencies in France who loyally accepted the conditions of the Peace of Frankfurt, who sought to repair their losses in other ways and wished to live at peace with Germany. Occasionally they were even countenanced officially. But they were always an object of suspicion to the Nationalists, regarded by them as traitors in disguise to the most sacred feelings of the French nation, and at decisive moments they could be thrust aside by an easily-roused popular agitation. . . .

As Bismarck's policy aimed at the maintenance of peace, it was of urgent importance for him to prevent any political disturbance of the peace either by the latent problem of Alsace-Lorraine, or by the open problem in the Near East. Hence two of the leading features of his policy must be to isolate France as much as possible so as to make a war of revenge out of the question, and to induce Russia and Austria to come to a settlement in the Near East, or at least to prevent them from coming to an open breach.

In order to isolate France it was advisable for Germany to get into touch as closely as possible with those states upon whose alliance France might count in the event of a war of revenge, among them Russia, Italy, and Austria. Even after 1871 there was a strong desire on the part of Austria to regain the position she had lost in 1866 should a favorable opportunity occur. A revival of the old coalition of the days of Frederick the Great — France, Austria and Russia — which Bismarck had long dreaded, was by no means so improbable as it seemed to a later generation. The League of the Three Emperors in the seventies, later on the Austro-German Triple Alliance, and the various treaties of security with Russia, all served a common end. An understanding with England was more than once considered, particularly during the Eastern crisis of 1875–1879, but all efforts failed because Bismarck stipulated for unconditional guarantees for the occupation of Alsace-Lorraine, and to this English statesmen would not consent. Even when they came into sharp conflict with France in 1882 over the occupation of Egypt, they were not to be won over. Towards the close of the eighties, when France and Russia began to draw together, Bismarck again proposed in London an alliance with England, sanctioned by Parliament, for mutual defense against an attack by France. He laid stress at that time on the fact that the knowledge that such a treaty existed would of itself be instrumental in preventing war. Lord Salisbury, who was then foreign secretary, was inclined to favor this suggestion. But some months later, when Count Herbert Bismarck was sent to London by his father to negotiate the Samoan question, and took the opportunity of mentioning the possibility of an alliance, Lord Salisbury held distinctly aloof. He reminded him of the parliamentary control of English policy and of the influence of public opinion which would not be easily won over to an alliance.

In spite of these efforts to isolate France, Bismarck's policy

towards the latter was in no sense hostile. He wished to prevent
France from disturbing the peace and from undoing the terms of
the Treaty of Frankfurt, and he endeavored to establish as friendly
relations as possible between Berlin and Paris. He went so far as to
assure France of Germany's active support in all questions where
their mutual interests did not conflict and to consent to her conquest of Annam and Tonquin. He encouraged France in her occupation of Tunis and repeatedly drew her attention to Morocco as a
suitable field for her colonial activity. He hoped that a successful
colonial policy would in some measure satisfy the French love of
prestige, and that the new colonial empire would in time provide
compensation for Alsace-Lorraine, so that possibly in the course of
a few decades the thought of revenge might die out. He himself well
knew that this was but a slender hope. Nevertheless he intended to
leave nothing undone that could tranquillize and conciliate.

R. W. Seton-Watson

À Trois in a World Governed by Five

Robert William Seton-Watson won an international reputation as an authority on Eastern Europe. Throughout his life he was sympathetic to
the cause of the Slavic peoples and during World War I helped win for
them the right of national self-determination. In the 1930s, moreover,
he published what is still one of the best accounts of British foreign
policy during the nineteenth century. While the focus of the work is the
diplomacy pursued by Downing Street, the author pays tribute to the
astute statesmanship of Bismarck, emphasizing particularly its effect
on the position of England in the Mediterranean.

Source: From R. W. Seton-Watson, *Britain in Europe, 1789–1914: A Survey of Foreign Policy*, 1937, pp. 501–502, 549–550, 563–565. Reprinted by permission of the Cambridge University Press.

It is hardly necessary to point out that the eclipse of France in 1870 completely altered the distribution of forces in Europe, and ushered in the period of "Armed Peace." The achievement of German unity under the auspices of Prussia, sealed by the annexation of Alsace-Lorraine, left Germany predominant on the Continent; France, exhausted by her defeats and by sanguinary civil dissensions, found herself completely isolated abroad, and the legend of her decadence was widely disseminated and believed. In Austria-Hungary the French defeats determined the failure of the federalist experiment, and the fall of the Francophil Beust, who was succeeded as Foreign Minister by Count Julius Andrássy, meant not merely the triumph of the Dual System and a virtual Hungarian predominance inside that system, but in foreign policy the beginnings of a rapprochement with Germany which was eventually to develop into the Triple Alliance. Meanwhile Spain had long since ceased to be a great power, while Italy was still consolidating her new position. Thus Britain's attitude in the war of 1870 had resulted both in her own isolation and in the temporary eclipse of the Western and Liberal powers as a serious factor in the European balance. But parallel with this there was a revival, in the years following the war, of the old alliance of the three Eastern Courts — the Three Emperors' League, as it was now called — a combination wellnigh irresistible so long as it held together. In its essence, it stood for the same ideals of conservatism and authoritative government as the earlier Holy Alliance — toned down, it is true, in Germany and Austria-Hungary to meet the requirements of the time, but none the less effectually resting upon dynastic control of military and foreign affairs — opposed to popular control wherever possible, and united by a further bond in the common necessity of preventing the resurrection of Poland. . . .

Without entering upon an analysis of the Bismarckian policy, it is possible to reduce its essentials to three fundamental axioms — at all costs to prevent a Franco-Russian alliance such as might force Germany to fight on two fronts, and at all costs to avert any situation in which it might be necessary for Germany to choose between Russia and Austria-Hungary, since a contest between these two powers might result in a war *à outrance* and in such a dislocation of forces in Eastern Europe as would be excessively dangerous to Germany. General dynastic and conservative principles, as well as common interests in the Polish question, increased still further his desire for a triple accord. "All politics," he told Shuvalov, "reduce themselves to this formula: Try to be *à trois* in a world governed by five powers. I have made an *entente à deux*, in order to return thereafter to an *entente à trois* if you really wish it. . . . "

The astute Bismarck was fully aware of Salisbury's dilemma, and spared no pains to draw Britain into the orbit of the Central Powers, thereby killing two birds with one stone, since he was raising the value of a renewal of the Triple Alliance in the eyes of both Vienna and Rome. Already on 12 February [1887] a secret convention was concluded between Britain and Italy, by which the two powers undertook to uphold the *status quo* in the Mediterranean, Adriatic, Aegean and Black Seas, while Italy accepted the British position in Egypt and Britain bound herself to the support of Italy in the event of "encroachments" in North Africa by another power which, though not named, could only be France. In signing such a document the British government gave to Italy

> the widest guarantee which any parliamentary state could give, namely, that in the event of a Franco-German war England would actively join that group of states which forms the peace police in the East. No English government can give an absolute guarantee for military or naval cooperation in a future conflict, simply because it is not certain whether Parliament will fulfill those promises. But so far as Lord Salisbury can judge he is convinced that England, jointly with Austria and Italy, will make front against Russia, if Turkey and especially Constantinople should be threatened. He thinks he can assume the same, but less certainly, if Austria is attacked by Russia, without touching Turkey. In this case it would be hard for England to give effective support.

This document should finally dispel the legend of Salisbury's belief in isolation, and it is confirmed by his private correspondence with the queen, from which it transpires that he had made it quite clear to Count Corti that "England never promised material assistance in view of an uncertain war, of which the object and cause were unknown," and again, that there never could be any question of Britain taking part in an aggressive war against France.

Austria-Hungary speedily announced her adherence to the Mediterranean Agreement, and later in the year it was rendered still more precise by a triangular agreement between London, Vienna and Rome, for the maintenance of the *status quo* in the Near East, and for joint action to prevent any cession of territory by Turkey, even to the point of provisional occupation of Turkish territory. Meanwhile Spain had entered into a special agreement with Italy to maintain the Mediterranean *status quo,* and not to lend herself to any action aimed against Italy, Germany and Austria-Hungary.

At this stage Bismarck, who from the background had never ceased to encourage the three Mediterranean participants, addressed himself directly to Salisbury, and after laying great stress upon the defensive character of German armed power and on the impossibility of any change upon the Imperial throne deflecting the fundamental lines of German policy, reached the conclusion that France and Russia were the two unstable elements in Europe, and that Germany would always be obliged to take action, "either if the independence of Austria-Hungary were threatened by Russian aggression, or if England or Italy were in danger of being set upon by French armies." Salisbury in his reply went boldly to the root of the matter by considering the contingency of a Franco-German war. In that event he credited Russia with a seizure of the straits, a step from which Britain and Italy alone "would not be sufficient to deter her," and "all would depend, therefore, on the attitude of Austria," who without German help could hardly risk war with Russia. His closing phrase ran,

> The grouping of states which has been the work of the last year will be an effective barrier against any possible aggression of Russia, and the construction of it will not be among the least services which Your Highness has rendered to the cause of European peace.

Salisbury was clearly reassured by this correspondence, following as it did upon Bismarck's revelation of the secret clause of the first Austro-German Treaty of 1879; for he had drawn from it the conclusion that "Germany *must* take the side of Austria in any war between Austria and Russia." Needless to say, however, he — and with him all the world, including the government of Vienna — was kept in ignorance of the secret "Reinsurance Treaty" which Bismarck on 18 June 1887 had signed with Russia. Bismarck, it is true, never admitted the charge of perfidy afterwards levelled against him, and definitely wished that the tsar should reveal the treaty to Francis Joseph. But it remains the crowning example of Bismarck's uncanny skill in juggling with four or five conflicting forces, and could not permanently have been kept up by any successor of lesser caliber. It would at any rate seem probable that Bismarck had finally disabused himself of his former suspicions towards Salisbury, whom he had described to St. Vallier at the Congress of Berlin as "ce clergyman laïque obstiné et maladroit."

It is thoroughly characteristic of Bismarck that no sooner had he secured the renewal of the Triple Alliance and reinforced it by the Mediterranean Agreements, than he once more proceeded to woo Russia, as he had done after concluding the Austrian Alliance in 1879. As ever, the key to his policy was his "permanent dread" of an Austro-Russian war, in which he would have to choose between his two allies and to risk the actual collapse of one of them. In the words of Dr. Gooch, "from the crisis which broke up the Dreikaiserbund and brought Austria and Russia to the brink of war, the chancellor's genius extracted securities for the empire he had founded, purchasing the assurance of Russian neutrality in a war provoked by France, by a promise of German neutrality in a war provoked by Austria." The long-drawn Bulgarian crisis enabled him to court Russia more openly than ever before. While all Bulgaria rallied behind the regents in their resistance to Russian dictation, and after no less than eighteen unsuccessful offers of the crown at last secured the acceptance of Prince Ferdinand of Coburg (a young cousin of Queen Victoria and a grandson of Louis Philippe), Bismarck pressed his Russophil orientation to the length of imposing a veto on the marriage of ex-Prince Alexander with the German crown prince and princess's favorite daughter Victoria, lest this should trouble Russo-German relations. In his Reichstag speech of 11 January 1887 he quoted, "'What's Hecuba to him?' What's Bulgaria to us?" The friendship of Russia was of far greater value, and above all else peace must be kept between Russia and Austria-Hungary. A year later, in the same place (6 February 1888), he balanced his absolute trust in the Tsar's word against the danger of coalitions, and declared, "Think of Austria off the map, and we are isolated, with Italy, between Russia and France. We cannot think Austria away." It was on this occasion that he closed with the memorable words, "We Germans fear God and nothing else in the world." To Frederick III on his deathbed he insisted that the "focussing point" of German policy lay in Russia and in preserving the personal friendship of Alexander III.

Fritz Fischer

The Continuity of German Aggressiveness

Church history was Fritz Fischer's first scholarly interest, but his experiences during the Third Reich as a soldier and prisoner of war, as well as his subsequent visits to England and the United States, turned his attention to the forces that had led his nation to disaster in the twentieth century. He began to study German diplomacy in the period 1914–1918, concluding on the basis of intensive archival investigation that the same tendencies toward aggressiveness and expansionism had characterized his country's policy in both world conflicts. This view did not endear him to conservatives and jingoists in his country, but the evidence he advanced in support of his contention is impressive. At the beginning of his major work on World War I, Fischer identified deep-rooted nationalism, militarism, and authoritarianism as the sources of Germany's catastrophic statecraft.

The German Empire created by Bismarck in 1871 was a partnership between the Prussian military and authoritarian state and the

Source: Reprinted from *Germany's Aims in the First World War* by Fritz Fischer, pp. 3–8, by permission of W. W. Norton & Company, Inc. Copyright 1961 by Droste Verlag and Druckerei GmbH, Dusseldorf. Translation copyright © 1967 by W. W. Norton & Company, Inc.

leading circles of the new industrial and commercial liberal bourgeoisie. It is true that, as a new nation state, it was one of a whole series of such entities which came into existence between 1789 and our own day; yet it occupied a position of special importance in the history of nations. The Germans were the only people who did not create their state from below by invoking the forces of democracy against the old ruling groups, but "accepted it gratefully" at the hands of those groups in a defensive struggle against democracy. The Prussian state, the power and prestige of the Prussian crown, the constitution which made the Prussian king German Emperor and the Prussian Prime Minister Chancellor of the Reich, the composition of the Prussian Diet (a Lower House elected on a restricted franchise and an overwhelmingly feudal Upper House), the bureaucracy, the schools, the universities, the established Protestant churches and not least the armed forces, directly subordinated as they were to the kings of Prussia, Bavaria, Saxony, etc. — all these were factors which guaranteed the predominance of the conservative elements against the pressure of the rising forces of democratic liberalism and later of democratic socialism.

The "Holy Roman Empire of the German Nation" which succumbed to Napoleon in 1806 consisted of more than three hundred principalities and Free Cities. In the German Confederation (*Deutscher Bund*) created to succeed it by the Congress of Vienna, and presided over by the new Austrian Empire, this number was reduced to about thirty, amalgamating the smaller units into "secondary states." This federation never satisfied the German people, who tried in the revolution of 1848 to create "unity and liberty" from below under the inspiration of west European ideas and on the model of the American federal constitution. But the liberal bourgeoisie was defeated by its own weaknesses and by its own dread of red revolution, which drove it into alliance with the princes. Another reason for the failure to achieve national unification lay in the rivalry between the two leading states in the federation, the Austrian Empire which sought to defend its position by the "*Grossdeutsch* solution," and the rising economic and military power of the kingdom of Prussia, with its "*Kleindeutsch* solution." The struggle for hegemony in Germany between the Catholic Hapsburgs and the Protestant Hohenzollerns was won by Prussia, under Bismarck's guidance, in the war of 1866 against a majority of the German states. Prussia then broke up the federation, excluded Austria from the future Germany, and extended its own power position by annexing the duchy of Schleswig-Holstein (detached from Denmark in an enterprise conducted jointly with Austria as recently as 1864), the kingdom of Hanover, the electoral principality of Hesse-Cassel, the duchy of Hesse-Nassau and the Free City of Frankfurt-am-Main, and by founding the North German Federation (*Norddeutscher Bund*) in 1867. This unification was thus created from above, but it was accepted by the majority of the liberal bourgeoisie, even though it meant the renunciation of democracy and parliamentary life in the Western sense.

Our description of Germany's war aims policy between 1914 and 1918 will show that the efforts to create a "Mitteleuropa" (like the Dual Alliance between the new German Empire and Austria-Hungary, which was formed in 1879 and lasted until 1918) were in a certain sense attempts to undo the decision of 1866 (subject, indeed, to Prussia's retaining hegemony over Austria). After breaking France's resistance to the incorporation of south Germany and annexing Alsace-Lorraine in 1870-1, Bismarck took advantage of the power position achieved in 1866 to incorporate south Germany in the new Reich, with the king of Prussia as German Emperor. This empire was a federation, composed of twenty-four member states: four kingdoms (Prussia — with five-eighths of the total area — Bavaria, Württemberg and Mecklenburg-Schwerin), six duchies, six principalities and three Free Cities (Hamburg, Bremen and Lübeck).

The federal element, which Bismarck utilised in order to attract the south German states of Bavaria, Württemberg, Baden and Hesse to Prussia and north Germany, undoubtedly helped the survival and development of the variety of German cultural life, as evidenced for example by the operas, theatres, concert halls, academies and museums of Munich, Stuttgart, Dresden, Weimar and Hamburg; but politically federalism counted for little in the decisions which were taken by the German Empire under Prussian leadership with Berlin, itself a cultural centre of the first rank, as capital both of Prussia and of the Reich. The representation of the federal states in the Federal Council (*Bundesrat*) — in which Prussia was the most strongly represented state — had little effect on the policies of the Imperial Chancellor.

Under the imperial constitution the Emperor appointed and dismissed the Chancellor at his discretion. The Chancellor, who was the only imperial official, was politically "responsible" to the Reichstag, before which he had to defend imperial policy; it had, however, no influence over his appointment, and he could not be a member of it. The Reichstag, as the national representative body, had the power to accept or reject the budget, and a voice in imperial legislation. The Chancellor had therefore to collect enough support among the parties to give him a majority; if he failed to do so, he had to dissolve the Reichstag and seek his majority at the polls. Foreign and military policy and decisions over war and peace were expressly reserved as prerogatives of the crown, which exercised them through the Chancellor. There was no imperial ministry responsible to the Reichstag, which could neither appoint a ministry, nor force it to resign by outvoting it, nor was there any collective Cabinet responsibility; the heads of the imperial ministries or "offices" (*Ämter*), who were known as Secretaries of State, were subordinate to the Chancellor, and were appointed and dismissed by the Emperor on his advice.

Another factor which strengthened the position of the crown and was calculated to restrict the Chancellor's power to determine policy was that the Prussian army (in time of war, also the armies of the other federal states) and the imperial navy were under the direct authority of the monarch. He exercised this authority through his military and naval cabinets (for questions of personnel) and through the general and naval staffs; the Chancellor had no voice in these questions, nor was there any co-ordinating machinery (the person of the monarch excepted) whereby the political aspects of military decisions could be given their proper weight. The Prussian Minister of War (who also represented the armies of the other federal states *vis-à-vis* the Reichstag) and the Secretary of State of the imperial Naval Office were concerned only with the recruiting and equipment of the armed forces, and with sponsoring the vote for them in the Reichstag; that body's influence over the army and the navy was limited to the indirect control which it enjoyed through its right to be consulted over the budget, but this right was restricted by the fact the vote was not annual, but was given for seven years at a time from 1874 to 1893 and for five years after 1893.

Another factor limiting the Chancellor's freedom of action was that (as a rule) he doubled his office with that of Prussian Prime Minister. In the latter capacity, however, he was only *primus inter pares* among the Prussian Ministers of State, who, like himself, were appointed and dismissed by the king, independently of parliament. This gave the Prussian state ministry considerable influence over the formation of Reich policy; the more so, since the restricted franchise ensured the preponderance of the conservative element in both Chambers of the Prussian Diet, while in the Reich the franchise was general, direct, secret and equal. The effects of the industrial revolution thus showed themselves in the growth of social democracy and of democratic and liberal groups, and this in turn widened the breach between political sentiment in the Reich and in its biggest individual state, Prussia.

Bismarck had expressly set himself to keep west European parliamentarism from establishing itself in the Reich or in its component states, and he was very successful in doing so. From 1867 to 1878 he conducted his internal and economic policy in partnership with the moderate, or "National," Liberals, known as "the Party of the Founders of the Empire." A radical change took place in 1878–9. Firstly, Bismarck abandoned free trade in favour of a "national" policy of protective tariffs on the American-Russo-French model for heavy industry and large-scale agriculture. Secondly, he began to relax the *Kulturkampf* which he had conducted since 1871 against the Catholic church and the Catholic party or Zentrum, and to draw that party over to support of the Prusso-German state by an accommodation with Pope Leo XIII and a new economic policy. Thirdly, in 1878 he opened his campaign against the Social Democrats (described by him as "the party of subversion") by emergency legislation directed against them, a course which he maintained until his fall in March, 1890. Under the policy of protection the old ideological parties — Conservatives, Liberals, Catholics — changed increasingly into bodies representing economic interests; the old landed aristocracy allied itself with the new industrial "aristocracy" against the opposition camp of Liberals and Social Democrats.

After the liquidation of the *Kulturkampf* the three parties of the right (German Conservatives, Free Conservatives and National Liberals) and the Zentrum, while not formally combining in a cartel, jointly represented the dominant forces, economic, political and social, in the new Germany, although it was not the Reichstag which made them dominant. The pull of this concentration of power, combined with an economic prosperity which had been steadily increasing since 1890 and the international nimbus and the growing power of the Empire, was so powerful inside Germany that by the close of the epoch even the two parties which had originally constituted the opposition, the left-wing Liberals and the Social Democrats, had come to accept the existing order, as August 4, 1914, and even November 9, 1918, were to prove beyond cavil.

The foundation of the German Empire greatly enhanced the national consciousness of the Germans. This new German self-consciousness was, in contrast to that of 1848, conservative and dynastic. After 1878 the liberal element in the German national movement was overshadowed by the dynastic and military elements. The popular consciousness regarded the foundation of the Empire itself, almost exclusively, as the fruit of three "victorious wars." The national festivals, the anniversary of Sedan symbolising victory over France, and the Emperor's birthday (he was born on January 27, 1859) were living expressions of this unreserved acceptance of the Empire.

One other factor, beside the military, coloured the nature of the new German national consciousness. In the '70s the campaign against liberalism and socialism led to the mobilisation of the *petite bourgeoisie* under the slogan (an old one, but re-furbished) of "throne and altar." This was the class which had been hardest hit by the new industrial developments, and was now hoping for help, especially help from the state, in its struggle to compete with the new big business. This mass feeling linked up with an anti-Semitism which was at first religious, then racial, and the fusion brought into being an entirely new kind of nationalism, which from 1890 onwards gave a wishful and emotional content to *völkisch* and racial conceptions which did not stop at the frontiers of the Prusso-German dynastic state. In 1881 the Union of German Students came into being as a part of this anti-Semitic movement, of which it soon became the most important mouthpiece. Founded with the purpose of providing the students' associations with an overall organisation and firing academic youth with the new German nationalism, and exerting considerable influence on the older rival student associations, corps and fraternities, it soon became a big factor in inclining the students' mentality towards the new dynastic-military, conservative and *völkisch* nationalism. The de-liberalisation of the Prussian bureaucracy and the nationalist spirit of the German Lutheran church are traceable to the same source.

The men of this generation which grew up in the late Bismarckian era were also convinced devotees of the "world policy" devoted to securing for Germany a "place in the sun," which the young Emperor had been quick to announce as his programme. It was the accession of Wilhelm II in July, 1888, that really unleashed the conservative-dynastic forces at home; those calling for pushful expansion abroad got their heads after the dismissal of Bismarck in March, 1890. This is not the place for yet another appreciation of the Emperor's character, but he was beyond question in many ways a typical product of his age. While entirely imbued with the concept that Monarchy came of Divine Grace, he was a "modern" king who sought contact with savants, merchants and technicians and, like the British Prince of Wales (afterwards King Edward VII), "covered" the world as "the first commercial traveller" of his people. Wilhelm II's insistence that Germany must not yield place to England coloured both his own political creed and the ideas of the great majority of his ministers and Secretaries of State.

William L. Langer

The Diplomacy of Checks and Balances

The works of William L. Langer of Harvard University are indispensable for an understanding of European diplomacy during the last decades of the nineteenth century. They present a careful historical

Source: From *European Alliances and Alignments*, 2/E, by William L. Langer. Copyright 1931, pp. 451–53, 503–5, 1950 by Alfred A. Knopf, Inc. Reprinted by permission of the publisher.

synthesis based on familiarity with a vast body of primary materials and secondary accounts in several languages. Langer has been criticized on some points, especially for his undisguised admiration of Bismarck's conduct of foreign affairs. But his views are supported by solid re-search, and although they should not be accepted as infallible, neither can they be rejected out of hand. Nowhere did the Iron Chancellor's extraordinary ability appear to greater advantage than in his mastery of diplomacy.

A more complicated chapter of diplomacy than that dealing with the year 1887 could hardly be found in the history of European in-ternational relations. And yet, though the clouds of war lowered on all horizons, the general peace was maintained. This fact alone is a tribute to the statesmen of the continent, most of whom desired to avoid conflict and showed but little sympathy with the violent out-bursts of national sentiment or the pressure for action exerted by the military men. But it may well be doubted whether the statesmen could have held their own against such pressure had it not been for the mastery with which Bismarck guided the course of diplomacy. It is easy enough to understand that many political and military writ-ers of the time regarded him as an evil spirit, a demon, an intriguer, a bully. They could not know what was going on behind the scenes, for the agreements made in this eventful year were secret. Had the chancellor had his way, they would probably have been public, as public as his great speeches, in which he reviewed the situation with the greatest bluntness, not to say brutality. Bismarck believed in an open diplomacy supported by strong national forces. He did not allow the military power of Germany to fall behind that of her neighbors, but he did not intend to use Germany's power for aggres-sive purposes. For him Germany was a "saturated" nation, forced to maintain a strong military establishment because of her dangerous geographical location.

As for his diplomacy, it was really simple in its underlying prin-ciples, and anyone might have understood it. Threatened on two fronts, Germany's interest was to prevent the formation of a

Franco-Russian coalition by showing herself amenable to Russian desires in Bulgaria, where Germany had no direct interests. The difficulty with this solution, however, arose from the fact that the Austrians and the Russians would not agree to a peaceful partition of the Balkans into spheres of influence. They threatened to go to war over the Bulgarian question. Now it was clear that in a Russian-Austrian conflict one of two things would happen. Either Russia would attack, in which event Germany would be brought in on Austria's side under the terms of the alliance of 1879; or Austria would attack and most likely be defeated unless Germany came to her assistance. But Germany could not afford to see the position of Austria as a great power jeopardized by a Russian victory. How was the dilemma to be solved? The Reinsurance Treaty is the key to the whole situation, for in it Bismarck, while securing Germany against the danger of a Franco-Russian alliance, checkmated the two eastern powers: Germany would stand by the party attacked. Thereby, as Bismarck put it, he had set a premium upon the preservation of peace.

There was only one great danger that haunted Bismarck after the conclusion of the Reinsurance Treaty, and that was that Russia, counting on German neutrality if Austria were the aggressor, would provoke the latter into taking the initiative. What would Germany's position then be? This difficulty was to be solved by the Mediterranean coalition, which in its earlier form was to ensure the three powers, England, Austria, and Italy, against the disturbance of the *status quo* in the Mediterranean. The agreement of December 12 represented a great reinforcement of the earlier understanding and made Russian action in the east almost impossible. She could no longer provoke Austria without coming to blows with the Near Eastern Triplice. Quite naturally, she chose to retreat in the Bulgarian question.

In all this there was no question of loyalty or disloyalty on Bismarck's part, any more than there was a question of his siding with one power as against another. Historians who attempt to make out a case of this sort in one way or the other are bound to find themselves in a blind alley. The German chancellor repeatedly distinguished between a policy of interests and a policy of prestige. He was following the interests of Germany, nothing more, nothing less. But above all he based his policy upon real factors in European relations. He did not expect others to act contrary to their own interests. Just as he would not engage Germany in a quarrel with Russia over Bulgaria or take the side of Austria in a Balkan policy which did not concern Germany, so he avoided unreasonable demands upon other powers. If the Austrians wished to fight because of Bulgaria, well and good, but let them first assure themselves of the proper support. Did the English wish to smash the Franco-Russian coalition in the Egyptian question and resist the Russian policy in the east at all costs? Let them do so, but let them first make the necessary arrangements with Austria and Italy, countries which had similar interests. In the same way the Italians should enlist the aid of the other Mediterranean powers if they hoped to check the French policy in North Africa.

One can hardly escape the conviction that Bismarck throughout this critical year, while doing his utmost to liberate Germany from the danger of a Franco-Russian alliance, at the same time maintained a careful balance between the other powers. He deluded and disappointed some and enraged others, Austrians as well as French and Russians, but he preserved the peace. Had he not been there, the nations would have had it out in the good old way. They had often fought on less pretext. But for Germany's sake Bismarck desired to avoid any conflict in Europe. He would not fight himself, no matter how favorable the situation might be for Germany, but at the same time he would not let the others fight if he could help it. As the situation stood at the end of 1887, no power could move without involving itself in endless difficulties and dangers. The sanctions of peace lay in the great alliance system which spread over Europe like a huge web. Bismarck was denounced and misunderstood, but for him the preservation of peace was worth it. . . .

His had been a great career, beginning with three wars in eight years and ending with a period of twenty years during which he worked for the peace of Europe, despite countless opportunities to embark on further enterprises with more than an even chance of success. No other statesman of his standing had ever before shown the same great moderation and sound political sense of the possible and the desirable. Of course much had changed since the time when he first took over the control of Prussian policy, and it cannot be said that he succeeded entirely in estimating the new forces at their full value. In the last years of his régime the old cabinet diplomacy had become quite impossible, for the dissemination of education and more liberal representative institutions had made public opinion a force in foreign affairs. Bismarck himself had not been much influenced by this new factor, for the German Reichstag had little to say in matters of international relations, and the chancellor, with his "reptile fund," was to mold press opinion to suit his needs, especially in cases of army appropriations. He had a very keen appreciation of the strength and danger of popular passions in other countries, but he was often unwise and unscrupulous in the way in which he manipulated German opinion and aroused the feelings of other nations.

It might also be said that the great chancellor failed to understand all the implications of the great economic changes that were taking place in Europe. The technical advances in armaments he saw clearly enough and he had no hesitation in joining the race for military power without making any serious effort to check the disastrous development of a Europe armed to the teeth. But his advocacy of a colonial policy was hardly more than reluctant and half-hearted. Even though he realized the growing importance of overseas sources and markets, he was, to the end, primarily a continental statesman. In the same way he allowed himself to be carried away by the wave of protection that swept Europe towards the end of the century, yet without seeing the great importance of close economic connections between Germany and her allies, let alone countries like Russia. The force of international finance escaped him almost completely until the very last years of his chancellorship, and by that time it was almost too late to check the course of events.

It must be remembered, of course, that no other statesman of his time was able to grasp the full significance of these tremendous changes. Bismarck at least deserves full credit for having steered European politics through this dangerous transitional period without serious conflict between the great powers. Paradoxically enough it may be said that by preserving the peace of Europe the great chancellor made possible the phenomenal development of forces which made peace more and more difficult to maintain in the future. As for his own diplomacy, its methods changed while its purposes remained the same. In 1871 he was certainly an advocate of the free hand in international relations. To bind oneself beforehand for certain eventualities that might never occur seemed to him contrary to the fundamental principles of good statesmanship. And yet when he laid down his offices, he had built up the most complicated system of alliances that Europe had ever known in peace times. It was, of course, the product of circumstances, the resultant of the new forces and the new pressure in international relations.

What his alliances came to in the aggregate was a series of security pacts designed to protect the German Empire from any conceivable attack so far as human foresight and ingenuity could do so. With the exception of a slight nuance in the German-Italian treaty of 1887 these agreements were all strictly defensive and were intended to secure the European center from aggression by the wings. To say that Bismarck's object was to isolate France is only a simplification of his policy and a half-truth. His object was to reduce the pressure upon the German frontiers as much as possible by diverting the European powers to colonial fields and by building up a system of protective agreements that made action difficult and dangerous. Realizing full well that the ferment and urge for expansion in a nation like Russia could not be wholly suppressed, he was willing to protect the Russian rear while the Russians were busy in Asia. He was willing even to allow them a reasonable field for expansion in the eastern Balkans. It was only because Austria, which was absolutely necessary to Germany to complete the Central European dike against Russia, objected to Russian activity even in Bulgaria that the German chancellor was led into the policy of the Mediterranean coalition. This combination, as viewed from Berlin, was designed for the simple purpose, not of checking the Russian advance in the Near East, for which Bismarck cared nothing, but of securing for Austria the support of England and Italy in protecting interests for which Germany was unwilling to fight. It was the classic illustration of Bismarck's uncanny sense for the objects and interests of other nations as well as of Germany. The Mediterranean coalition was a tool in Bismarck's hand, but it was not based on unfair exploitation of the other powers. Quite the contrary, the chancellor simply brought together powers like England and Austria who had been for years groping in the dark to join hands.

Bismarck in the Reichstag. The Iron Chancellor appears here delivering his famous speech of February 6, 1888, in which he declared defiantly, amid wild applause, that "we Germans fear God and nothing else in the world!" Many of his countrymen used to love that kind of bombastic rhetoric. (Archiv für Kunst und Geschichte, Berlin)

PART

V The Iron Chancellor

Hans-Ulrich Wehler

A Bonapartist Dictatorship

Most German historians writing since World War II agree that the empire created by Bismarck perpetuated civic loyalties and traditions that ultimately led their country to catastrophe. No one else has advanced this thesis with greater vigor or cogency than Hans-Ulrich Wehler of the University of Bielefeld. Relying on the techniques of the social sciences, especially sociology, Wehler has argued that national unification was achieved under conditions that promoted economic progress but retarded political modernization. There is a historic continuity, in other words, extending from the establishment of the empire in 1866–1871 to war and defeat in 1914–1918 and to dictatorship and genocide in 1933–

Source: From Hans-Ulrich Wehler, *The German Empire, 1871–1918* (Leamington Spa and Dover, NH: Berg Publishers, Inc, 1985), pp. 55–62. Reprinted by permission of Berg Publishers.

1945. For Wehler, Bismarck is not the Iron Chancellor but the evil genius of Germany.

The liberals, who had finally succumbed to *Realpolitik* between the time of the Constitutional Conflict and the founding of the Empire at Versailles, were willing to put up with "Bismarck's bold tyranny . . . in the interest of creating the Empire." But after a few years of National Liberal influence on legislation and an equally pronounced self-deception as to their own worth, critical thinkers in their midst began to speak of the "brutal rule of an omnipotent *Junker's* frivolous and whimsical notions" as a "chancellor dictatorship." This concept was not understood in an exact constitutional sense in the 1870s and 1880s, of course. As all its critics were aware, the subordinate position occupied by the Imperial Chancellor was laid down unequivocally in the constitution. But as a description of constitutional reality, the term readily suggested itself, with the result that even the historian Friedrich Meinecke viewed the German Empire's first chancellor as exercising "a kind of dictatorship." In fact, there can be little doubt as to this dictatorial element. Whether from the left or right of the political spectrum, well-informed contemporaries who knew those involved agreed on this point. "Everything depends entirely on Bismarck" was the judgement of the ultraconservative German ambassador in St. Petersburg, General von Schweinitz: "There has never been a more complete autocracy." He saw the guiding motto of "Bismarck's dictatorship" as being *Moi, je suis l'état.* That "everything hinges on Bismarck," was also the view, based on close observation, of the later Secretary of State and Minister of Education, Bosse: "He has the ministers completely on a leash." "Under the rule of this Jupiter," complained the Mecklenburg delegate to the Federal Council, Oldenburg, "everything carried on in the correct rhythm and proffered dumb obedience . . . everyone placed himself without fuss under the yoke." "Old Liberals" like the Rhenish entrepreneur Mevissen regarded Bismarck as having been "omnipotent for some time." The "Prince's absolutism stood at the zenith of its power and presumption," and the liberal Friedrich Kapp mocked bitterly that "Bismarck acknowledges only one form of government: himself." He needed only "a majority of eunuchs" in the *Reichstag* "who would not be allowed to open their mouths." Foreign observers like the English ambassador, Lord Ampthill, spoke in equally clear terms of a "German dictator whose power is at its height." The American minister John A. Kasson, spoke of "an effectively all-powerful dictator" whose "prestige at present is without parallel in European history." These judgements were echoed several times over by the French diplomats St. Vallier and de Courcel. As if further proof was required even Kaiser Wilhelm I confessed: "It isn't easy to be an emperor under a chancellor like this one." Against the entire spirit of the constitution, but in a revealing Freudian slip, his remark that "Your subjects [i.e., ministers and imperial secretaries of state] must possess your confidence," revealed the true hierarchy in Berlin. "I am master of Germany in all but name," was how Bismarck with reputed candour described in exact terms his skilfully feigned role as a "vassal of Prussia."

Nevertheless, the concept of a "chancellor dictatorship" is still not enough. It is too narrow and personalistic. For a comparative typology of forms of political rule, which can accommodate the constitutional reality of imperial Germany, the concept of Bonapartism is particularly useful. Its explanatory value in illuminating the social function of political authority is to be found in its peculiar combination of charismatic, plebiscitary and traditionalist elements, all of which were also clearly in evidence in Germany. Deriving from the regime of Napoleon III, and classically analysed in Marx's *Eighteenth Brumaire*, Bonapartism is best understood as an authoritarian form of government which first appeared in a relatively early phase of industrialisation when the pre-industrial élites were still able to demonstrate their strength; the bourgeoisie was making rapid advances, while simultaneously threatened from below by the workers' movement — foreshadowed by the "red spectre" of the revolutionary years of 1848 to 1849. It would be quite misleading, however, to speak of an equilibrium existing between the major classes. The traditional power structure, hitherto based on estates, was being challenged at this time. The bourgeoisie was being strongly moved by the fear of social upheaval into accommodating itself with the forces of tradition. It renounced its claim to the direct exercise of political power at a time when the workers were arousing fears as a force for modernisation, or at least as a symbol for change. In the light of such a specific constellation of forces, often viewed as an open-ended state of "suspension," extraordinary opportunities could open up for a charismatic politician to carry out a policy of stabilisation on behalf of the ruling classes by the use of certain devices appropriate to the times. Historical examples show that these always involved a mixture of limited compromises, including surprising concessions to progressive demands (suffrage, welfare measures, commercial legislation) on the one hand, and blatantly harsh repression and persecution of opponents (the anti-Socialist laws, press gagging, deportations) on the other. It also meant diverting pressures for emancipation at home into the sphere of foreign affairs by means of either a militant political adventurism abroad or a policy of imperialism. The threat of revolutionary measures (*coup d'état*, mobilising of national minorities) or their actual implementation (suffrage, territorial annexations) was also ever-present. It was this last characteristic that distinguished Bonapartism from traditional conservatism, as Bismarck's conservative mentor, Ludwig von Gerlach, was to discover. With the help of this combined strategy, sanctioned at the polls by plebiscitary approval, the traditional and the industrial élites strengthened their position of predominance once more (although the latter had to accept certain political limitations). Moreover, the position of the pre-industrial élites was prolonged beyond its appropriate life-span in a society in which powerful social changes were at work. The dictatorial rule which emerged in this situation was widely accepted, indeed demanded, by the ruling class on the grounds of its need for protection. For a time it was able to achieve a relative balance between the various powerful social forces at work; it even attained a certain degree of independence in the face of the existing configuration of power relationships. In many ways it was fighting a desperate defensive campaign against the social and political consequences of Germany's industrialisation. In terms of its social effects, this rear-guard action meant — in the short term in other countries, but in Germany in the long term — a socially conservative, anti-emancipatory obstruction of modernisation throughout German society, allowing for no more than partial change.

Bismarck fitted into this scheme as the representative of the traditional ruling élites and the "saviour" of the "law-abiding middle class." Engels was thinking of the latter in particular when, after the

coup of Bismarck's electoral law in April 1866, he drew a general
conclusion in his perceptive analysis of conditions in France:

> *Bonapartism is indeed the true religion of the modern bourgeoisie. It
> is becoming increasingly clear to me that the bourgeoisie does not
> have the will to rule directly, and so . . . a Bonapartist semi-dictator-
> ship is the normal form. The great material interests of the bour-
> geoisie carry this through, even against the bourgeoisie's own wishes,
> but it does not let them have any share of political power. At the
> same time, this dictatorship is itself forced in turn to adopt the
> bourgeoisie's material interests against its will. So now we have
> Monsieur Bismarck adopting the programme of the National
> Union (Nationalverein). Putting this into practice is another
> thing, of course, but Bismarck is scarcely likely to fail with the Ger-
> man bourgeois.*

Indeed, Bismarck did not fail. He not only fulfilled the German
bourgeoisie's economic aspirations and protected it from the restive
proletariat, but consolidated the position of the traditional ruling
élites which, in the light of history, proved to be no less successful.
His cooperation with the National Liberals who advocated Free
Trade may have temporarily deceived them as to the true nature of
his "semi-dictatorship"; but his regime revealed itself blatantly after
the onset of the second world economic crisis in 1873. From 1879
onwards it became even more obvious than ever. Up until that
point Bismarck's regime had been favoured by the social and political framework in which it operated: a rising economy, relatively low
political participation and weakness in the political parties *vis-à-vis*
the bureaucracy. We should not, therefore, make too much of
Bismarck's undisputed skill as a politician. From 1879 onwards,
however, as a result of changing circumstances whose effects
caused him to turn his thoughts increasingly towards a *coup d'état*
(Staatsstreich), he found that his management of the system was becoming increasingly difficult.

Bismarck balanced traditional and modern elements in a combination that was typical of Bonapartism. For example, he combined
an absolutist-style military policy with state interventionism on behalf of vested interests and underpinned it by plebiscitary approval.
Through a policy of war up to 1871 and later, in the 1880s, of social
and economic imperialism, he sought to stifle internal problems by

diverting attention to the sphere of external affairs. Through it all he lived off an undeniable and heightened charisma derived from his role in the founding of the German Empire, his foreign policy and his successful mediation over a long period between the two dominant social classes. Ludwig Bamberger, one of the major liberal figures, concluded with grudging admiration after thirty years' proximity to Bismarck: "One had to have been there to be able to testify to the power this man exerted over all those around him at the height of his influence. There was a time when no one in Germany could say how far his will extended . . . when his power was so rocksolid that everything trembled before him." Not everyone possessed the ironic detachment which caused Burckhardt to remark that "in Germany . . . Bismarck was practically the reference point and yardstick for that mysterious thing we call authority." But even this conservative, who saw Bismarck's mistakes and weaknesses clearly, had to admit after the shock of the three revolutions of 1789, 1830 and 1848 "that there was no alternative in sight, wherever one cared to look, for carrying out the supreme task of stemming the tide of revolution." A clear-headed judgement will therefore conclude that "after 1862 Prussian-dominated Germany had found its Caesar." As the historian Heinz Gollwitzer put it:

> The "Bonapartist" character of Bismarck's policies was hidden beneath the cloak of monarchical tradition, which he wore as the King's servant and Imperial Chancellor with considerable decorum and skill. What distinguished him from earlier masters of monarchical government was the "modern" element in his political game, the "Bonapartist" ingredient. It was discernible in his recurring policies of risk-taking at home and abroad, in his manipulation of universal suffrage, his skills as an agitator, contempt for legitimacy, and the ambivalence of the conservative revolution.

In order, however, not to stress the personal element too much but, instead, slightly to modify Marx's analysis of the German Empire, it might be best described, for the period before 1890, as a Bonapartist dictatorship based on plebiscitary support and operating within the framework of a semi-absolutist, pseudo-constitutional military monarchy. It favoured the traditional élites, but was at the same time subject to a rapid industrialisation process with its effect of partial modernisation; it was thus to some degree influenced by the bourgeoisie and the bureaucracy. This definition accounts in full measure for Bismarck's position at the head of an informal pyramid of power and for the socially conservative function of his Bonapartist methods of rule.

Two further considerations arise. This Bonapartist phase derives its importance from the fact that it overlapped with the period in which the German Empire was founded. The turning-point of 1879 is of crucial importance in this connection. Although Bismarck cooperated up to this point with the liberals in domestic affairs, economic legislation and foreign trade policy, after 1873 the depression undermined first the economic, then the political foundation of this unstable alliance of forces. And yet it did not simply represent a *societas leonina* as far as the National Liberals were concerned. In tackling the problem of interruptions to industrial and agricultural growth the imperial government changed course after 1876. It began to pursue an anti-liberal, conservative regrouping of forces whose main support came from the major interests in industry and agriculture. This "cartel of the productive estates," as it was called, first emerged in spectacular fashion with the adoption of the protective tariffs of 1879. From then on, until 1918, variations of this type of conservative *Sammlung*, designed to rally major interests, were to form the basis of government policy. Parallel to this ran a policy of carrying out de-liberalisation measures in many different areas of political and social life. Since these developments were encouraged by Bismarck, and their consequences given the stamp of legitimacy by this enormous authority, a disastrous course was set prior to 1890 for the entire direction taken by the German Empire's subsequent historical development. For this reason, Bamberger, whose worldly-wise scepticism rejected any personality cult, concluded that "Bismarck has determined the course which institutions, the laws and — more important — which minds will follow." The first crucial dozen years of this *Sammlung* policy, which rallied agrarian and industrial interests, coincided with the era of Bismarck's Bonapartist semi-dictatorship and the supporting policies it adopted. These ranged from Puttkamer's policy for the civil service . . . to state social insurance schemes, from experiments with professional advisory bodies to advise the government on the national economy to overseas expansion. And all these policies paved the way, as early as the Bismarck era, for the emergence of an anti-liberal, authoritarian

German state. Hans Rothfels, in writing on the subject of the continued "obstruction to the development of civic responsibility" and "the glorification of excuses" in German politics, rightly concluded that, after 1945, "no matter how long and tortuous the road from Bismarck to Hitler," the first Imperial Chancellor seemed "to be the one responsible for the change in course, or at least its legitimisation, and one whose unfortunate progress towards its culmination in our own time has been only too apparent."

Bismarck's road to the twentieth century was in fact paid for by the immediate imposition of a massive burden on Germany's internal social and political development. . . . So far as the German Empire's social constitution is concerned, however, the impression was already widespread by 1890 that "the great man has produced a downright fiasco." Burckhardt noted that "he can no longer heal the Empire's internal wounds," and as famous an historian as Theodor Mommsen was even of the opinion that "Bismarck has broken the nation's backbone. The damage done by Bismarck's period in office is infinitely greater than the benefits it has brought. The gains in power will be wiped out in the next great upheaval of world history. But the oppression wrought [by the German variant of Bonapartism] was a disaster which can never be put right." Certainly, there is still much that will have to be said about this undeniable damage, but it should not obscure one fact: the new power structure, built up by the dominant classes and their *Sammlung* policy, began to function well enough in Bismarck's time and continued to do so without him, regardless of any frictions which might have existed. This became clear after 1890 when Bismarck's dismissal led to the disappearance of the "pilot" from Berlin and, hence, the symbol of Bonapartist rule.

Johannes Ziekursch

The Campaign Against Socialism

Few German academicians spoke out during the 1920s in defense of the ill-fated Weimar Republic. This reluctance of the intellectual leaders of the country to commit themselves to the democratic ideal contributed to its decline. But there was nothing pusillanimous about the stand taken by Johannes Ziekursch, professor of history at the Universities of Breslau and Cologne. His spirited account of the German Empire reveals a firm faith in the liberal creed. It charges Bismarck with the sins of authoritarianism and arbitrariness which brought the nation to disaster in 1918. The vain struggle against socialism, it maintains, reveals the Iron Chancellor's reliance on the mailed fist in dealing with those he could not cajole or frighten.

In the Reichstag elections of January 1877 the number of Social Democratic votes rose by 40 percent, from 352,000 in 1874 to 493,000. Only the National Liberals, the Center, and the Conservatives showed greater strength. To seven Saxon electoral districts and one Thuringian were added two in Berlin, one in Silesia, and one in the Rhineland. The number of Socialist Party newspapers grew from year to year with surprising rapidity. In 1878 there were already 75 of them, both large and small.

As early as the imperial press law of 1874 and the penal law of 1875 Bismarck had demanded weapons against this party, but without success. Nine days after Hödel's attempt on the life of the Kaiser an anti-Socialist bill was presented to the Reichstag at the insistence of the chancellor. The Free Conservative Minister of Agriculture Friedenthal and the Conservative Minister of Justice Leonhardt had vainly warned against the promulgation of an

Source: Johannes Ziekursch, Politische Geschichte des neuen deutschen Kaiserreiches, 3 vols. (Frankfurt-am-Main: Frankfurter Societats-Druckerei G.m.b.H., 1925–1930), Vol. II, pp. 325–333, translated by Theodore S. Hamerow and William W. Beyer.

exceptional law. The effect of such laws during the *Kulturkampf* had been apparent to all. But Bismarck replied that

> *we can only strike at the heart of Social Democracy if we are empowered to disregard the barriers which the [Prussian] constitution has established in the so-called fundamental rights, barriers arising out of an excessive, doctrinaire concern for the protection of the individual and the parties. In dealing with Social Democracy the state must act in self-defense, and in self-defense one cannot be finicky in the choice of means.*

Thus in a few days Privy Councilor Bucher in the Foreign Office drafted a law modeled after an English act of Parliament directed against the secret, revolutionary Irish Fenian Brotherhood. The law was very slipshod. Publications and associations pursuing the objectives of Social Democracy were to be prohibited, but the nature of these objectives was not clearly defined, so that, as Bennigsen pointed out in the Reichstag, even the most philanthropic activities and scholarly discussions could fall within this category. The Bundesrat, which met only from time to time and which voted according to instructions, was supposed to confirm or invalidate within four weeks every measure which the police had taken against Socialist publications, associations, and meetings. The decisions of the Bundesrat were to be considered by the Reichstag; 397 deputies of the most diverse political convictions, of whom only a fraction was trained in law, were then supposed to vote concerning the content, meaning, and danger of dozens of newspaper articles.

The National Liberal deputy from Leipzig Stephani concluded that the bill "is ostensibly directed against Social Democracy, but in fact against the National Liberals." "We are still not so frightened of the red specter," declared Hölder, a National Liberal from Württemberg, "as to sanction measures which we fought with all our strength when they were being promulgated by the late Diet of the German Confederation." On May 24, 1878, the Reichstag rejected the bill, after the National Liberals had declared themselves ready to support the government with an imperial law strengthening the provisions of state laws dealing with associations and assemblies. Even Bismarck's confidant, the head of his chancellery Privy Councilor von Tiedemann, admitted that the rejection of this anti-Socialist law was not unjustified.

Then on June 2, 1878, came a second attempt on the life of the Kaiser. An educated man of thirty, Dr. Karl Nobiling, the son of an estate manager in Posen, wounded the Kaiser so seriously that it was doubtful whether the octogenarian ruler would survive. For several months the crown prince had to take the place of his father. After his deed Nobiling tried to kill himself. Seriously wounded, he died three months later in prison. Nothing was known about any deposition he may have made, except that he was supposed to have subscribed to Socialist ideas.

When Bismarck in Friedrichsruhe received news of the assault, he exclaimed: "Now we will dissolve the Reichstag." He immediately reviewed all the political consequences of the attempted assassination, and only then inquired about the condition of the Kaiser and the details of the crime. He proposed to make good use of this unexpected incident.

The news of Nobiling's bloody assault on the monarch who had secured German unification and hegemony on the European continent after three glorious wars gave rise to wild indignation among the people. Rumors about attempts on the life of the crown prince and Prince Friedrich Karl, about plans to dynamite the palace in Berlin, and about the danger of a revolution in the capital flew about for the next few days. Monarchical loyalty and national pride condemned the ingratitude and public disgrace of Nobiling's outrage. Since both assassination attempts were immediately although mistakenly attributed to Social Democracy, popular anger turned against it. Feelings were intensified by fear of the dangerous forces of the underworld, which the public thought it had finally identified. Memories of the terrible days of the Paris Commune were awakened.

The economic ascendancy of the middle class since the founding of the Zollverein and the beginning of railroad construction had taken place in such a short time filled with great political struggles, and the economic difficulties of the last five years had been so serious, that the bourgeoisie had lacked the time and energy to concern itself with the condition of the industrial workers. The well-to-do found comfort in the doctrine of the harmony of economic life which alone would heal the injuries it had inflicted. They believed that government intervention in behalf of the workers could easily transform the economic crisis into a catastrophe. The workers were therefore urged to rely on their own strength and on the self-help to which the middle class owed its welfare, although under different conditions. Vainly had voices in the camp of the Clericals and the south German democrats appealed for social reforms. Vainly had after 1872 many scholars, the so-called "socialists of the chair," joined in the Association for Social Policy in order to awaken the public conscience and pave the way for reform by thorough scholarly research. The brusque, uncomprehending rejection of these efforts by Heinrich von Treitschke, the prophet of the German Empire, in his work on *Socialism and Its Patrons* exemplifies the attitude of the vast majority of the middle class. After the assassination attempts Treitschke's resounding condemnation of the Socialists seemed to most people entirely justified. The coarse, provocative tone which Socialist deputies, agitators, and newspapers had adopted in the past, and their constant threats of revolution now led to a terrible retribution.

Against the will of the majority of the Prussian ministry Bismarck forced the dissolution of the Reichstag, hoping to isolate the left wing of the National Liberals by intimidating the other members of the party. He rushed into the struggle not only against the Socialists, but also against the liberals. He let it be known everywhere that the Progressives could no longer be considered among the parties of order, and that there was no difference between voting for a Socialist and for a Progressive. Because of their occasional collaboration with the Progressives in elections the National Liberals were accused of indirect support of the Socialists. Then for the first time Bismarck began to think in earnest that a modification of the franchise or some change in the Reichstag and its constitutional position might be necessary. Not that he had until now considered the suffrage law inviolable. Almost immediately after its promulgation he had replied in the summer of 1867 to the warnings of district president von Diest in Wiesbaden: "If in a few years the system of election is no longer necessary, or if I do not like it any more, I will revoke it." The moment when he did not like it any more was about to come. On August 12, 1878, Bismarck wrote the King of Bavaria:

> *The purpose of the German Empire is the maintenance of justice. At the time of the establishment of the existing union of princes and cities parliamentary activity was envisioned as a means of achieving*

the purpose of the federation, not as an end in itself. I hope that the conduct of the [new] Reichstag will spare the associated state governments the need ever to act on the practical implications of this legal situation.

Besides the destruction of the Socialists, Bismarck demanded of the new Reichstag completion of the reform of imperial finances which was supposed to end contributions from the states and even provide a considerable surplus for them. In Prussia the lowest brackets of the class tax yielding 21 million marks, which in the days of economic crisis could in most cases be collected only by the bailiff, were to be eliminated, while half of the land and property tax amounting to 35 million marks was to be transferred to the municipalities. The trade tax paid by artisans and small shopkeepers was to be reduced by 2.5 million marks. Hobrecht, the new Prussian minister of finance, privately demanded an additional 60 million marks for other purposes. Thus for Prussia the new system would have to provide altogether about 120 million marks, for the other federal states 80 million, and for the empire 45 million, so that the reform was to bring in approximately a quarter of a billion marks. With such hopes and promises did the government enter the election campaign which was decided at the end of July and in August 1878.

In the election 360,000 more voters went to the polls than in the preceding year. The Socialists, nevertheless, lost 56,000 votes or 11.3 percent of their total vote of 1877, while the National Liberals lost 150,000 votes or 10.4 percent, the Progressives and the Löwe faction 35,000 or 7 percent, and the Center 27,000 or 2 percent. The Conservatives gained 219,000 votes or 41.9 percent of the votes they polled in 1877, and the Reich Party gained 366,000 votes or 86.3 percent.

Accordingly the National Liberals declined from 127 to 98 seats, the Progressives and the Löwe faction from 44 to 31, and the Socialists from 12 to 9, while the Center suffered no losses and even increased its representation when its Guelph allies grew from 4 to 10. The Conservatives increased from 40 to 59 seats, and the Reich Party from 38 to 56. Now 129 liberals opposed 115 conservatives and 103 Clericals and Guelphs. The decisive role was no longer played by the liberals but by the conservatives, who could combine with either the liberals or the Center. Despite his opposition to the

National Liberals before the election, Bismarck invited them afterward to collaborate with the conservatives.

A much improved version of the anti-Socialist law was submitted to the new Reichstag. For example, appeals against police measures were no longer to be submitted to the Bundesrat and the Reichstag, but to a commission composed of four members of the Bundesrat and five judges under a chairman appointed by the Kaiser. Socialist meetings, parades, celebrations, and associations could be prohibited. Professional agitators who had violated the law might be expelled by court order from specified towns and districts, but expulsion from their place of domicile was to be legal only if they had resided there less than six months. Those agitators who were innkeepers, printers, booksellers, and lending librarians could be barred from practicing their occupation, while in districts exposed to danger martial law might be proclaimed. Furthermore, all meetings had to be approved in advance by the police, the sale of publications on the streets and the possession of arms could be prohibited, and persons who presumably endangered public safety could be exiled.

The premature disclosure of the draft of the anti-Socialist law deprived Bismarck of the chance to add even more rigorous restrictions. He wanted, for example, the right to dismiss Socialist civil servants without a pension, for he clearly recognized that

> the majority of the poorly paid minor officials in Berlin, and then the railroad signalman, the switchman, and similar categories are Socialists, a situation whose dangers may become evident in times of insurrection and in the transportation of troops. I believe, moreover, that if the law is to be effective, then it is impossible in the long run to allow any citizen legally proved a Socialist to retain the suffrage, the right to run for office, and the enjoyment of the privileges of a member of the Reichstag.

Bismarck therefore came to the conclusion that "the bill as it now stands does no serious harm to socialism, and is altogether inadequate for its suppression."

At Lasker's suggestion the Reichstag limited the law to two and a half years, until the end of March 1881. Thereby the measure lost much of its effectiveness, while provoking the workers by the repeated debates in the Reichstag concerning its renewal. Because of this and other shortcomings Bismarck might perhaps have ordered another dissolution of the Reichstag, if the crown prince, who was still acting in the place of his sick father, had not opposed the plan. On October 19, 1878, the anti-Socialist law was passed by the votes of the Conservatives, the Reich party, the National Liberals, and the Löwe faction.

All the political parties had taken the same position as at the time of the first anti-Socialist law. Only the National Liberals and the supporters of Löwe had yielded to the pressure of popular excitement after the assassination attempts. The National Liberals understood the significance of their about-face. Their *Korrespondenz* wrote at the time:

> No one fails to recognize that the suppression of revolutionary aspirations will not be without effect on civic freedom in general. As long as we are engaged in a struggle against the Socialist mortal enemy, any further development of the constitutional state can certainly not be considered.

Such was the end of the confident belief which had prevailed since 1866 that political unity had to be achieved first, because then the liberal development of the empire would inevitably follow. With the anti-Socialist law the liberal bourgeoisie rejected the workers, just as it had completely embittered the Catholics by the *Kulturkampf,* and provoked the Conservatives through the reform of the Prussian administration without weakening them. The liberal era ended at about the same time that Bismarck thought he had won leadership among the European Great Powers at the Congress of Berlin. For he felt that he could finally dispense with the support in domestic affairs on which he had hitherto relied. The anti-Socialist law thrust a thorn into the flesh of the German people; a festering wound was opened which still has not healed to the present time.

Jürgen Kuczynski

The Empire as Capitalist Exploitation

Jürgen Kuczynski was an ardent Marxist; he joined the German Communist party while still in his twenties. Forced during the Third Reich to seek refuge abroad, he returned after the war to become the best-known historian in the German Democratic Republic. His lifework was the study of labor conditions under industrial capitalism, especially in Germany. Although subtlety and understatement were never Kuczynski's strong suit, he amassed a vast body of useful statistical data pertaining to the standard of living of factory workers. His contention that while the nominal wages of the urban proletariat rose during the German Empire, the profits, dividends, and rents of the propertied classes rose even more is quite persuasive.

In Germany, the situation was considerably more complex than in France. While Britain had already passed through the critical phase when the 1848 revolution broke out in France, Germany had not yet entered it. At the same time, a conflict was fermenting in Germany for other reasons: . . . a clash between the politically suppressed bourgeoisie and the semi-feudal Junkers. Engels says rightly, in *Revolution and Counter-Revolution*, that the French revolution "hastened" the German revolution. It definitely came earlier than was required, if we consider solely the methods of capitalist production and their compatibility with the general productive forces of society. Society was not yet in a state of revolt against the specific methods of capitalist production. But it would have soon come anyway, if not for "internal capitalist" reasons, then because of the conflict between the capitalist bourgeoisie and the semi-feudal Junkers, a conflict in the specific economic field as well as on

Source: Jürgen Kuczynski, *A Short History of Labor Conditions under Industrial Capitalism: Germany, 1800 to the Present Day*, pp. 113–115, 141–144, 154–155, 173–174. Published by Frederick Muller Ltd., 1945, London.

the question of the distribution of power between Junkers and bourgeoisie.

It is not surprising, therefore, that the partial economic solution in the clash of forces of the bourgeoisie and the Junkers brought by the revolution of 1848 sufficed to bring about an extraordinary upswing of production during the fifties — still with the old methods of production and exploitation, but with greater freedom for industrial capitalist methods of production to develop and with fewer feudal barriers. Nor is it surprising, therefore, that the revolution brought no marked change in the methods of production and exploitation. The great change in the methods of capitalist exploitation and production occurred, to a widely noticeable degree, only in the sixties — in form of an economic revolution from above, combined with a national revolution from above. And the full development of this second phase in the history of German capitalism took place only after the unification of Germany into a nation, after 1871. The period from 1871 to 1900 is the phase of the rapid maturing of German capitalism, the phase in which, as Engels says, Germany grew into an industrial country of the first rank.

A few figures are sufficient to indicate the rapid development of German economy in the period from 1871 to 1900. This development, it should be emphasized, was due to two factors: the new methods of production and exploitation, applied to some extent already during the sixties, and the consummation of the attempts of the German bourgeoisie and not inconsiderable sections of the Junkers to unite the German states into a national entity.

The wars of the sixties and the first part of the war against France were wars for the unification of Germany and their success led to the formation of the German Reich. The constitutional unification of the Reich was followed slowly but surely by a unification of numerous economic and legal institutions. In the course of time one monetary unit was created in Germany, numerous commercial legal practices and laws were made uniform, and so on. It is obvious that these measures contributed very considerably to the rapid development of German national economy.

The most comprehensive index of national economic activity at our disposal is the index of production. The following table gives an index of industrial and agricultural production per head of the population by trade cycles since 1860.

Physical Volume of Industrial and Agricultural Production per Head of the Population, 1860 to 1902

(1900 = 100)	
Trade Cycle	Index
1860–1867	53
1868–1878	62
1879–1886	70
1887–1894	82
1894–1902	102

The rate of growth from one trade cycle to another was remarkably stable; it fluctuated between 15 and 20 per cent and was only slightly higher in the last cycle, when it almost reached 25 per cent. The question arises: how did the rise in industrial production compare during this period with that in the preceding one with its other methods of production and exploitation? If we compute averages for two trade cycle periods (or two decades in former periods), we arrive at the following table.

It is not surprising that the rate of growth of the first few decades of industrial capitalism was not maintained, for in the early phases the erection of a few factories had already influenced the growth of production. What is surprising is the high rate of increase

Industrial Production During the Nineteenth Century

(1913 = 100)	
Trade Cycle	Index
1801–1820	1
1821–1840	3
1841–1860	9
1860–1867	15
1868–1886	25
1887–1902	49

during the last third of the nineteenth century and especially during the last 15 years. . . .

A very important element in the changed methods of exploitation of the working class was a rise in real wages during the period from 1870 to 1900. This rise was necessary if the employers wanted to increase the intensity of work per hour and still keep the workers in a state of health which enabled them to go on working. If, in the years from 1900 to 1914, real wages did not continue to increase, this was definitely not due to a change in the trend of the intensity of work but rather a result of a "total and desperate effort" of the ruling class to raise profits by all available means, regardless of the consequences (not for the proletariat because about that they have never bothered but) for the working forces at their disposal. If we call the period of monopoly capitalism and imperialism the period of capitalism in decay, such terms include also the recklessness and irrationality which characterize the thoughts and actions of a moribund body.

During the period from 1870 to 1900 the wages of a small stratum of workers — small as compared with the rest, but not so small in itself — of the labour aristocracy in the process of formation, rose more rapidly than those of the mass of the workers. During the first fourteen years of the twentieth century, this relative improvement in the position of the labour aristocracy stopped as regards wages; if there was any change in their relative position it was probably for the worse. But this refers only to wages; the ruling class found other means to persuade at least part of the labour aristocracy to assume the role of reformists and compromisers.

If we measure wages by what was officially regarded as a normal budget for an industrial worker's family (but what we regard as an insufficient minimum), we find that they were insufficient and no trade-cycle average reached even this poor standard. The widening of the gap between wages and the budget during the twentieth century is actually greater than the figures indicate, as they do not take into account the need for a higher standard because of the increased intensity of work.

As to relative wages, we find that they decline from trade cycle to trade cycle over the period from 1870 to 1900 as well as during the twentieth century. Relative wages are the only kind of wages which declined continuously, regardless of the specific methods of exploitation and the various phases of capitalist development. The relative position of the workers like their absolute position, declines continuously under capitalism. But while the absolute deterioration takes place in various forms — sometimes also with real wages and purchasing power increasing — the decline in the relative position of the workers (though not, of course, its actual extent) can always be observed from a study of relative wages alone, which . . . have always gone downwards.

As wages are only one of the factors determining the working and living conditions of workers, we will now study the other factors shaping their standard. In this study we must give special attention to the period from 1870 to 1900, in order to discover what are the factors over-compensating the increase in purchasing power of the workers.

The new phase in the history of labor conditions — that is, the change in the methods of exploitation which the sixties brought about — referred not only to the development of wages but also to many other factors, very prominent among them being the development of the hours of work. It is the decline in the number of hours of work, probably even more than the gain in real wages, which enables the employers to increase productivity and intensity of work per hour — partly through a more drastic driving of the worker per hour without any important changes in the place of work, partly through a reorganization of the production process (more machines for one worker, Taylor system, etc.), and partly through the installation of improved machinery.

The decline in the number of hours worked per day could have been noticed here and there in the fifties, following the revolution of 1848; but the effect of the revolution with respect to hours was very small indeed, and it is doubtful whether an index of hours of work per full time week would have been lower in the fifties than in the forties. Moreover, the fifties brought a rapid expansion of industrial production while in the forties many years were years of crisis. It is possible that even if in the fifties there was in some branches of industry a slight decline in the number of hours worked per normal working week the individual worker worked longer on the average than in the forties.

The sixties brought a radical change in this respect. The number of hours worked per week showed a general tendency to decline.

Only two branches of national economy were excepted from this — most of the agricultural occupations and industrial work performed at home. I believe that as far as capitalist home work is concerned, the number of hours worked per day has remained roughly the same during all the years of its existence. We find the 14, 15 and 16-hour day being worked at home in 1825, in 1875, and in 1925. The only changes in this respect applied in the first place to children who, because of the enforcement of school attendance, were freed for at least part of the day; and, secondly, the greater fluidity of labour enabled home workers in good years to obtain other work, and thus to vary their 100-hour week periods with others of shorter working weeks. As to agricultural work, no decisive change took place until after the revolution of 1918; that is, during the whole period under review the number of hours worked remained almost stationary: in 1910 the agricultural worker worked about the same hours as in 1860, and in 1860 about the same as in 1830.

For all other groups of workers the working day began to decline. This was most rapid in the better organized industries. Again an indication of the fact that, while they cannot change the structure and periods of capitalist development, the trade unions are able to accelerate certain processes. . . .

The very great increase in the productivity per worker which took place between 1860 and 1910 is the result of improved machinery and organization of the working process, and of increased intensity of work. While the first two factors represent definite progress, the third is one of the main items adversely affecting the standard of working and living of the workers. Real wages increased during the major portion of the period reviewed. Hours of work declined during the whole period under review. If, however, we relate these two facts to the increase in the intensity of work, we must not only regard them merely as pleasant counter-balancing factors but as the basis upon which the intensity of work was increased.

Without a shortening of the working day and more food for the increasingly exhausted workers, the intensity of work could not have been increased. Capitalism did not make an amicable gift of the shorter working day and improved real wages. But, rather in order to increase the rate of profit and to diminish the contradiction between the specific forms of early capitalist production and the productive forces, the capitalists were compelled to change their methods of exploitation, to concentrate on increasing intensity of work. This they could do only on the basis of a shorter working day and increased real wages. Even so, they made every effort to keep the working day as long as possible and the rise of real wages as small as possible. That real wages were increased to the extent shown, and the working day was shortened to the extent given, was due to the pressure of an increasingly well organized labour movement.

But what proof have we for the fact that the intensity of work actually increased? We have no statistics of the development of the intensity of work. We know, on the other hand, that this increase was a common experience during these years. But it would be much better if we had more tangible evidence than expressions by individual workers, especially as it is difficult to remember the intensity of work five or ten or twenty years ago even for a worker who has experienced the effects of these production methods. . . .

There is not the slightest doubt that the introduction of the system of social insurance improved the conditions of the sick, injured or aged workers. We have seen that about half of this improvement is due to the contributions from the workers themselves. The number of workers affected by accidents and sickness was greater after than before the introduction of the social insurance system; and those workers who in former times were not affected by these evils and were able to work, were better off than those who later received social insurance benefits. And this point must be kept in mind: the social insurance system was a palliative for evils which were affecting an increasing number of workers. Only if we realize this can we properly evaluate the social insurance system in a capitalist country. There are various ways to look at this.

First, such a system is infinitely better than no system at all.

Second, such a system is only a palliative for growing evils.

Thirdly, such a system under capitalism does not properly alleviate completely the evils against which it is supposed to protect the worker.

For these reasons it is important to realize that, while the significance of the progress in social legislation in Germany as compared with other countries before 1914 must be fully recognized, the extent of the advantages the worker obtained was not as great as might at first glance seem apparent.

Geoff Eley

The Mythology
of the *Sonderweg*

The thesis that Germany's descent into dictatorship and barbarism during the Third Reich resulted from a *Sonderweg*, a unique historical path
which that country had followed for more than two hundred years, was
challenged in the 1980s by two young British historians. David Black-
bourn and Geoff Eley argued that the course of political development
in Central Europe in the nineteenth century, although different from
that in Western Europe, had little to do with the rise of National Socialism in the twentieth century. In fact, the German bourgeoisie had the
same aspirations and could boast of the same achievements as the British or the French bourgeoisie. Thus, what happened under Bismarck
cannot account even indirectly for what happened under Hitler. This
iconoclastic view, defended here vigorously by Eley, attracted a great
deal of attention but not many converts among students of German
history.

[T]here were many reasons why a stronger parliamentary state on
the model of either the British or the French was unlikely to develop, whether we stress the economic, social, and religious divisions of the bourgeoisie itself, the formidable radicalism of an independent Social Democratic labour movement, or (and not least) the
residual aristocratic strengths entrenched defensively in the 1871
Constitution. But "parliamentarization" does not exhaust the possible forms of peaceful or relatively stable development for the Imperial German state as it entered the twentieth century. There is no
reason (again in the abstract) to assume a priori that a modified
or stabilized version of the Imperial state should be incapable of

meeting the needs of the emerging capitalist social order. Once we acknowledge that the "rule" of the bourgeoisie (as the dominant class in society) is exercised indirectly, we should also accept that in theory a wide variety of state forms is adequate to the task, from the most authoritarian (late forms of absolutism, fascism, and other forms of dictatorship) to the most democratic (the democratic republic, forms of the welfare state, types of social-democratic corporatism), depending on the society and period in question. Once we concede this, we can also acknowledge that intermediate combinations of the two (authoritarian and democratic) are a viable possibility.

In the light of this I am really trying to argue two things. First, the authoritarian features of the Imperial Constitution are not to be equated automatically with "archaism," "backwardness," or political inefficiency. Neither the exclusivist (the checks on popular participation), executive (the relative weakness of direct parliamentary control), nor aristocratic (privileges of the titular nobility) features of the political system were particularly unusual by the contemporary European standards of the later nineteenth century. In some ways the Second Reich seemed terribly "modern" to commentators elsewhere — in the technocratic efficiency of its bureaucracy and military machine, in its more interventionist state, in the vaunted excellence of its municipal administration, in its system of social administration, and (from a different point of view) in the existence of universal suffrage and the extent of popular political mobilization. Conversely, the other states of Europe were certainly not lacking in authoritarian features of their own, whether we look to the limited franchise and hereditary elements of the British Constitution, the extremely oligarchic character of the political system in Italy, or the more obviously absolutist systems further to the east in Austria-Hungary and Tsarist Russia. To say this is not to say that there were no differences between the *Kaiserreich* and Britain, or the *Kaiserreich* and Russia. But the respective stability of those states depended on the breadth, popularity, and cohesion of their social base, and the relative adequacy of their institutional apparatuses for organizing the necessary degree of consensus amongst both dominant and subordinate classes. And there is no reason why authoritarian features *per se* should render them totally disabled for this purpose.

Thus we can concede the Imperial state's authoritarianism without accepting the normal corollary, that it was inevitably condemned to some "permanent structural crisis." To put it another way, the authoritarian parameters of the Imperial Constitution allowed considerable latitude for manœuvre, negotiation, and compromise before the inner limits of the Bismarckian settlement (the prerogatives of the monarchy, the survival of the landowning aristocracy, and the social and economic power of the dominant classes) began to be breached. Within the same fundamental limits the Imperial state showed itself reasonably adaptable (certainly in the circumstances of its foundation, and for large parts of the subsequent four decades) to the tasks which a capitalist state is called upon to perform — securing the conditions of capitalist reproduction, doing the work of legitimation (in the Wehler-Habermas sense), organizing the unity of the dominant classes, mobilizing the consent of the people. In fact, I would suggest (this is the second argument I am trying to make) that the strictly reactionary elements were considerably more isolated in the political system, that the Constitution was considerably more flexible, and that "modernizing" forces had achieved considerably more penetration — indeed that the "traditional" elements were considerably less "traditional" — than recent historians have tended to believe. In particular, the common equation between authoritarian social and political structures, rightwing politics and imperialist foreign policies on the one side, and "backwardness," archaism, and "preindustrial traditions" on the other, is potentially extremely misleading. It may be, in fact, that precisely the most vigorous "modernizing" tendencies in the *Kaiserreich* were the most pugnacious and consistent in their pursuit of imperialist and anti-democratic policies at home and abroad. If this is so (or at least worthy of discussion), then perhaps we should think again about what exactly the "traditional" and the "modern" mean, both in general and in the specific context of the *Kaiserreich*.

What I want to suggest is that in the past we have had our starting-point wrong. If we believe that the German bourgeoisie missed the boat, that it failed to establish its social, cultural, and political ascendancy in a manner commensurate with the dominance of capital in the economy, that "pre-industrial traditions" survived when they should have been swept away, and that German industrialization unfolded within a framework of political institutions unsuited to the tasks of modernity — in short that the political system of the *Kaiserreich* was out of time — then that whole vocabulary of "secondary integration," "negative integration," "social imperialism," "manipulation," "Caesarism," and "plebiscitary dictatorship" becomes necessary to explain how the whole irrational system held together. If we believe that the Imperial state was so radically incapable of organizing consensus amongst the electorate, articulating the interests of the dominant classes into some workable basis of unity, co-ordinating the construction of social coalitions for the purposes of government, and generally integrating the divergent regional and economic sectors of the newly created German social formation, then the thesis of structural instability and the idea of a "permanent structural crisis" makes eminent sense.

If on the other hand we believe that the feebleness and subordination of the bourgeoisie have been exaggerated, that the degree of "positive" integration in Germany's social and political order was much greater, and that the "mixed" authoritarianism of the Imperial Constitution was less a sign of pathology than of rational fittedness to historically specific circumstances, then an alternative perspective begins to emerge. I have spent some time in this essay suggesting how one particular issue — that of industrial paternalism and the prospects for a decisive liberalizing departure before 1914 — might benefit from such a shift of perspective. I would argue further that we have reached the point in German historiography where future advances in our understanding of the Imperial period will require systematic exploration of this perspective from other points of view as well. This is the only way in which interesting new questions — as against the predictable rehearsal of old knowledge — will ever take shape. . . .

In bringing this essay to a conclusion — and to provide a basis for future discussion — it is worth formulating programmatically the main arguments I have been trying to make.

(a) First, we can make a reasonable case for arguing that Germany did, after all, experience a successful bourgeois revolution in the nineteenth century. This did not take the form of a pitched battle between bourgeoisie and aristocracy, in which the former seized state power from traditional monarchy and replaced it with parliamentary democracy. But then it didn't anywhere else in Europe either, certainly not in Britain in the seventeenth century, and certainly not in France in 1789. This view of the bourgeois revolution, where the insurgent bourgeoisie triumphantly realizes its class interests in a programme of heroic liberal democracy, is a myth. But if we associate bourgeois revolution with a larger complex of change — instead of a narrowly defined political process of democratic reform — which cumulatively established the conditions of possibility for the development of industrial capitalism, then there are good reasons for seeing the process of "revolution from above" between the 1860s and 1870s as Germany's distinctive form of the bourgeois revolution, so that we focus more on the material or objective consequences of events than their motivational origins. We have to accept that the national forms of bourgeois revolution may vary considerably, and certainly can't be identified straightforwardly with either the British or French examples, not least because the latter are themselves in serious historiographical dispute. In other words, the German pattern of "revolution from above" (spanning the two concentrated periods of 1807–12 and 1862–71) was just as capable of ensuring bourgeois predominance as the different developmental trajectories of Britain, the United States, or France. This leaves open the question of whether "bourgeois revolution" is the best term for describing this process. In this essay I have preferred to retain it. But the argument would stand perfectly well in its absence.

(b) Secondly, on this basis, rather than stressing the reactionary qualities of the Bismarckian settlement and the "capitulation" of the liberals, we should accept the broadly "progressive" character of German unification. I mean this in two specific senses, neither of which is, I trust, too teleological: on the one hand, to refer to the conditions of existence of the emergent capitalist mode of production, the institutional consolidation of the national market, and a German-wide process of industrialization; on the other, to invoke the characteristically bourgeois vision of a new social order as that was understood at the time, by enemies and exponents alike. The new Empire was certainly not the summit of constitutionalistic perfection, let alone the enthronement of liberty (but where was?). But between 1867 and 1873 liberal demands for national institutions and constitutional regulation, national economic integration, and the rule of law became the centrepiece of the new constitutional settlement, which consummated the process begun by the *Zollverein* (Customs Union) several decades earlier. Moreover, behind this political achievement were deeper processes of institutional growth and cultural coalescence — the outwardly visible side of the bourgeoisie's class formation — which brought bourgeois notabilities to regional, municipal, and local predominance, and allowed liberals to stake their claims to moral leadership in society ("hegemony," in Gramsci's sense). The *Kulturkampf* — literally a struggle to unlock the potential for social progress, to free the dynamism of German society from the "dead hand" of archaic institutions — perfectly expressed this combative unity of social, cultural, and political aspirations. This general buoyancy of the liberal presence in the political culture of the 1870s, and the liberals' straightforward domination of the state governments, the Reichstag, and the content of Bismarck's legislative programme, belies the usual view of liberal demoralization and ineffectuality. In other words (to adapt a phrase), the German bourgeoisie was very much present at its own making, and liberalism supplied the materials of its construction.

(c) Thirdly, it is quite wrong to see the bourgeoisie under the German Empire as being somehow politically weak or "immature," or as failing by some obscure criteria to realize its collective interests as a class. In any case, it is both theoretically misconceived and empirically impossible to view the bourgeoisie as a single intersubjective unity in this way, because politically (though not economically or sociologically) there can only be different tendencies within the bourgeoisie, which in different situations may achieve a higher or lower degree of cohesion. But more specifically, this hides the fact that the interests of the bourgeoisie (or more exactly, the different fractions within it) may be pursued and secured by other than liberal democratic means. In other words, it is necessary finally to accept that the Imperial state between 1871 and 1918 was actually compatible with the adequate realization of legitimate interests and aspirations of the bourgeoisie. The *Kaiserreich* was not an irredeemably backward and archaic state indelibly dominated by "preindustrial," "traditional," or "aristocratic" values and interests, but was powerfully constituted between 1862 and 1879 by (amongst other things) the need to accommodate overriding bourgeois capitalist forces.

(d) Following on from this, we need to re-evaluate both the origins and significance of the Second Empire's evident "authoritarianism" (i.e. the limited extent of its parliamentary-democratic development). This partly requires a revision of theoretical perspective. German "authoritarianism" was not unavoidably bequeathed by an iron determinism of "pre-industrial continuities," but was specifically overdetermined by the evolving disposition of forces within the German social formation as it entered its predominantly capitalist phase — above all by the simultaneous coexistence of significant aristocratic enclaves within the structure of the state and a powerful Socialist labour movement in German society, and by important contradictions between different fractions of the bourgeoisie. The complex interaction of these factors produced a high degree of fragmentation and instability in the post-Bismarckian power bloc — the coalition of dominant social forces on which effective government had to depend. This was exacerbated during and after the 1890s by the appearance of sharper contradictions amongst the dominant classes (setting industry against agriculture, protectionists against free traders, manufacturers against primary suppliers, small against big capital), and by the persistent volatility and independent mobilizations of the subordinate classes. This made it difficult to construct the necessary degrees of internal unity and popular support which the dominant classes needed to effect a genuinely organic relationship to government. This situation — which elsewhere I tried to characterize as a dual difficulty of the power bloc, a prolonged crisis of its internal cohesion and hegemonic capability — helps explain both the government's relative independence from a stable parliamentary bloc in the Reichstag for most of the period 1890–1914 and the heavily segmented appearance of the German party system. While this did not necessarily prevent the political system from functioning, it did have the effect of seriously inhibiting the putting together of a sufficiently powerful liberal reformist coalition before 1914, in ways which I tried to discuss above.

Thus in tackling the problem of "Germany's persistent failure to give a home to democracy in its liberal sense" (Dahrendorf), we have to be extremely clear about exactly what kind of question we are asking, because in previous discussions two distinct problems are frequently confused. On the one hand, there is the question of the conditions under which a bourgeois capitalist society could successfully reproduce itself, or to put it another way, the legal, political, and ideological conditions of existence for a successful German capitalism. Then on the other hand, there is the question of how a more liberal political system might have been achieved. *These are not the same question.* To take an example discussed extensively above, there can be no disputing that the practices of the most powerful fractions of German capital before 1914 were extremely reactionary by most of the standards we have become accustomed to after 1945. But whether they were really in conflict with the needs of capitalist reproduction is a very different matter. To put this more positively, it may be that such practices owed far more to the special circumstances of the industries concerned (in the ways dealt with earlier in this essay) than to the influence of any "pre-industrial" mentalities.

(e) Next, it is worth drawing attention to a problem of rather surprising neglect amongst German historians, namely the area of social policy in the broadest sense. This is the point at which the two problems distinguished in the previous paragraphs — the legal, political, and ideological preconditions for a viable capitalist society, and the chances for a more liberal political system — begin more clearly to separate. For the unstable dialectical unity of bourgeois interests and liberal politics held together quite successfully in the 1860s and 1870s; it was mainly in the 1880s and particularly the 1890s that things fell apart, so that liberal conceptions of the parliamentary state and the bourgeoisie's capacity for reproducing its social domination began to diverge. In the space that opened there crystallized a distinctive field of public activity, some of it centralized in agencies of government, some borne by different kinds of civic initiative, which aimed at regulating and organizing the new social environment of a rapidly industrializing and urbanizing economy. This encompassed everything from social investigation (e.g. the statistical movement, the public-health movement, the *Verein für Sozialpolitik*, and so on), to specific movements of social reform (housing reform, poor law, town planning, local financing, public health), educational activity of different kinds, processes of professionalization, and the more obvious areas of labour legislation (accident and sickness insurance, provision for old age, factory inspection, labour exchanges, unemployment provision, and so on). The point about this type of activity is that in practice it was concentrated in the city, and proceeded regardless of the liberal parties' parliamentary fortunes. In fact, the impressive accomplishments of German municipal administration were articulated only very ambiguously with the concerns of parliamentary liberalism. This was an authentic domain of bourgeois political achievement, in other words, that owed nothing to the existence of a liberal democratic state. It was perfectly compatible with the latter, but certainly did not require it. . . .

In general, this is an argument against notions of German exceptionalism. It suggests that we should think again about the assumed absence of bourgeois revolution in nineteenth-century Germany and accept that the bourgeoisie may come to social predominance by other than liberal routes. Finally, it is meant to query the simple continuity thesis which locates Germany's vulnerability to fascism in a "pre-industrial" blockage of "modernization." On the contrary, it might now be far more useful to examine the particular forms of German capitalist development and the new structures of politics they helped broadly to determine. In other words, Germany's failure to develop a native liberalism of comparable vitality to that of Britain may have lain more with the conditions of capitalist reproduction themselves than with the continuing domination of a "pre-industrial power élite." At least this is worth discussing.

"Dropping the Pilot." The author of this political cartoon, which appeared on September 2, 1890, in the London satirical weekly *Punch*, was Sir John Tenniel, famous as the illustrator of *Alice in Wonderland*. It shows an old and embittered Bismarck leaving the ship of state, while the youthful William II looks on in total indifference. (Bildarchiv Preußischer Kulturbesitz, Berlin)

PART

VI

The Bismarckian Legacy

Friedrich Meinecke

A Synthesis of Power and Culture

When Friedrich Meinecke embarked on his academic career, the great Leopold von Ranke was still writing his vast history of the world. When he died in 1954 at the patriarchal age of ninety-one, his fame was nearly equal to that of the great nineteenth-century master. The reputation he had won rested on a series of brilliant studies that sought to analyze the underlying ideas of modern political life. After World War II the grand old man of German historiography published his reflections on the

Source: Friedrich Meinecke, *The German Catastrophe: Reflections and Recollections,* translated by Sidney Bradshaw Fay, Copyright © 1960, pp. 10–15. Reprinted by permission of Harvard University Press.

tragic era in which he had lived, urging his nation to return to the humane ideals of its classic age.

In the Prussian state of Frederick William I and Frederick the Great there lived two souls, one capable of culture and the other hostile to culture. The Prussian army as created by Frederick William I brought forth a remarkably penetrating militarism that influenced all civil life and found its like in no neighboring state. However, as early as the travel sketches of Montesquieu, who lived in Hanoverian territory near the Prussian frontier, we find some unpleasant things about it. The question of the origin of Prussian militarism we can leave to one side; we wish to inquire here only into its influence on German destiny as a whole in the nineteenth century.

As long as the synthesis of intellect and power seemed to look hopeful in the nineteenth century, we regarded even militarism with a more benevolent eye; we emphasized the undoubtedly high moral qualities which were evident in it: the iron sense of duty, the ascetic strictness in service, the disciplining of the character in general. Easily overlooked, however, was the fact that this disciplining developed a leveling habit of conformity of mind which narrowed the vision and also often led to a thoughtless subserviency toward all higher authorities. This habit of conformity caused many of the richer springs of life to dry up. Furthermore, the advocates of Prussian militarism overlooked at first the fact that all sorts of unlovely practices and passions could rage under cover of exterior discipline. Public life also might suffer from these effects of militarism if the statesmen and generals, who had grown comfortably important in the militarist atmosphere, had an influence on the life of the nation. This evil seemed apparent even at the time of the War of Liberation, when the synthesis of intellect and state was for the first time boldly attempted. The synthesis was in many ways brilliantly attested, but ultimately was fatally crippled by a militarily narrow-minded monarch and by an equally narrow-minded and at the same time egotistical caste of nobles and officers. The crippling of the reform movement, symbolized in 1819 by the dismissal of Wilhelm von Humboldt and Boyen, may be regarded as a victory in the Prussian state of the soul that was hostile to culture over the soul that was capable of culture. The rift ran straight through the whole nineteenth century and was inherited by the twentieth century. Finally, Prussian militarism also secured a large place for itself in the mixing pot into which Adolf Hitler threw together all substances and essences of German development which he found usable.

However, in the era when the empire was founded, the aspects of Prussian militarism which were bad and dangerous for the general well-being were obscured by the imposing proof of its power and discipline in its service for national unity and in the construction of Bismarck's empire. The military man now seemed to be a consecrated spirit — the lieutenant moved through the world as a young god and the civilian reserve lieutenant at least as a demigod. He had to rise to be reserve officer in order to exert his full influence in the upper-middle-class world and above all in the state administration. Thus militarism penetrated civilian life. Thus there developed a conventional Prussianism (*Borussismus*), a naive self-admiration in Prussian character, and together with it a serious narrowing of intellectual and political outlook. Everything was dissolved into a rigid conventionalism. One must have observed this type in countless examples with one's own eyes in the course of a long life, one must have felt it in one's own self, struggled with it, and gradually liberated one's self from it, in order to understand its power over men's minds — in order to understand finally the effect of the touching comedy in the Potsdam church on March 21, 1933, which Hitler played with Hindenburg beside the tomb of Frederick the Great. For here National Socialism was expected to appear as the heir and propagator of all the great and beautiful Prussian traditions.

A man like Theodore Fontane, whose lifework represents as none other all that was great and beautiful in the Prussian tradition, could, in a letter written in 1897, near the end of his life when he had grown critical and keen of insight, utter words of displeasure about the Prussian world around him. His testimony is not to be rejected simply because it is sharply exaggerated in every direction. "Borussism," he wrote, "is the lowest form of culture that has ever existed. Only Puritanism is still worse, because it is completely given to lying." And another time he wrote: "What must be crushed first of all is militarism."

This evil Borussism and militarism was like a heavy mortgage imposed on Bismarck's work and inherited from him by his hybrid successor, Hitler. There was, however, also something in the immediate contribution of Bismarck himself which lay on the border between good and evil and which in its further development was to expand more on the side of evil. The truth of this criticism would never be readily conceded by those who grew great under Bismarck's work and richly enjoyed its blessings. We Germans often felt so free and proud, in contrast with the whole previous German past, in this mightily flourishing empire of 1871 which gave living space to every one of us! But the staggering course of World War I and still more of World War II makes it impossible to pass over in silence the query whether the germs of the later evil were not really implanted in Bismarck's work from the outset. It is a query which courageous and unfettered historical thinking must pose in regard to every great and apparently beneficent historical phenomenon in which a degeneration takes place. One then breathes the atmosphere of the tragedy of history, of human and historical greatness, and also the problematical uncertainty which will ever hover around a Bismarck and his work — while Hitler's work must be reckoned as the eruption of the satanic principle in world history.

Consider now the year 1866 and Bismarck's blood and iron policy. Today we listen with more emotion to the voices which at that time expressed concern over the great evils of the future — voices of such important men as Jakob Burckhardt and Constantin Frantz, and one might add as a third the queer Swabian, Christian Planck. Bismarck's policy, according to them, was destroying certain foundations of Western culture and the community of states and was a really deep-reaching revolution which was opening the prospect of further revolutions and an era of wars. It meant, they said, the victory of Machiavellism over the principles of morality and justice in international relations and it let perish the finer and higher things of culture in a striving after power and pleasure.

Let us be honest. However one-sided these complaints may have been, there is a grain of truth in them. On the other hand, there are plenty of voices to defend Bismarck. They call attention to all the similar examples of Machiavellian practices in the rest of Europe of that day and especially to the fact that Bismarck himself recognized limits to his policy of force. These defenders likewise point out that in his peace policy after 1871 Bismarck did good service to the Western community of nations. "You know I cannot love Bismarck," a Danish historian friend said to me during the Third Reich, "but now I must say; Bismarck belongs to *our* world."

One must regard Bismarck as a borderline case. He still had in mind to some extent the conception of a synthesis of power and culture as it was understood by the leaders of the movement for German unity. These leaders themselves, with Treitschke at their head, originally were seriously offended by Bismarck's first steps in the period of the constitutional conflict, but became his defenders and admirers as a consequence of the war of 1866. The result was that in the synthesis of power and culture, of the things of the state and the things of the spirit, the preponderance slowly but steadily shifted further over to the side of power and its domain. From my own development I can bear witness to this — until, in the years before the First World War, a reaction of humanitarian feeling once more began to set in.

One can always object that the power-state and Machiavellism were not confined to Germany, that they were more often preached but not more strongly practiced by us Germans. This view is quite true. Specifically German, however, was the frankness and nakedness of the German power-state and Machiavellism, its hard and deliberate formulation as a principle of conduct, and the pleasure taken in its reckless consequences. Specifically German also was the tendency to elevate something primarily practical into a universal world-view theory. It was a serious thing for the future that these ideas about power-state and Machiavellism, at first expressed merely as theories, might become practical weapons in the hands of ruling authorities. The German power-state idea, whose history began with Hegel, was to find in Hitler its worst and most fatal application and extension.

The degeneration of the German people is what we are here trying, by groping and probing, to understand merely in its rough outlines. How difficult it is, however, to sketch a picture of the spiritual and cultural condition of Germany in the first decades after the founding of the empire in 1871, of the good as well as the bad germs in it! The judgment commonly expressed today, often merely parroting Nietzsche, that liberalism had become flat and shallow, settles nothing. The silver age of classical liberalism, of which we spoke, still persisted and still produced in art and science much that was brilliant, while the average level and everyday taste remained decidedly low. But no one then would have thought possible the emergence in educated Germany of a phenomenon like National Socialism — only the uneducated, proletarian Germany of Social Democracy was feared as a serious menace to our culture in the future. We, especially we younger Germans, felt exceedingly safe, entirely too safe, in the possession of a high national and cultural heritage.

Gerhard Ritter

The Last Great Cabinet Statesman

The traditionalist school of German historians found a brilliant spokesman in Gerhard Ritter. A student of Hermann Oncken, he wrote prolifically on nearly every period of the history of Central Europe from the age of scholasticism to the resistance against Hitler in which he himself had participated. It was his contention that the political institutions of Germany cannot be judged by the standards prevailing in Western Europe. They must be understood in the light of the unique historical experiences that have formed the outlook of the Germans. As for National Socialism, it was not the expression but an aberration of the national spirit. A new democratic Germany would do well to reexamine the older and sounder tradition evident in the statecraft of the Junker from Schönhausen.

The liberal and democratic popular movement of 1848 had shown itself in practice powerless to create a new German national state

Source: Gerhard Ritter, *Europa und die Deutsche Frage: Betrachtungen über die geschichtliche Eigenart des deutschen Staatsdenkens*, pp. 77–86, © 1948 F. Bruckmann KG, Munich. Translated by Theodore S. Hamerow and William W. Beyer. Reprinted by permission of the publisher.

against the opposition of the princely governments and the particularism of a large proportion of the German people. Not only armed force, but also the monarchical, conservative sentiment of sizable groups of the population, primarily though not exclusively in the eastern provinces of Prussia, had made the triumph of the reaction possible. The Habsburg state, hardly recovered from internal upheaval, had used threats of war reinforced by foreign alliances to undo the last, timid efforts of Prussia to save at least a part of the work of unification by peaceful agreement among the monarchical governments. Only under a particularly favorable constellation of the European powers could German nationalism risk a new attempt in this direction. For it had been demonstrated that Europe was not ready to accept the establishment of a new, large, national state in its midst without opposition. The danger of intervention by the great neighboring powers was all the more serious, because the Habsburg monarchy was obviously determined to reassert its old hegemony over Germany and to defend it in bloody conflict, if need be, against Prussian claims to leadership.

That is how the situation looked, and that is how Bismarck understood it. When at his first public appearance as minister he announced that he did not believe that the German problem could be solved in any way but through "blood and iron," he only meant to express this sober judgment, rejecting the visionary hopes of his liberal opponents that Prussia could achieve the leadership of a united Germany by a policy of "moral conquests," that is, by winning the support of public opinion. That he was essentially correct, in other words, that without an armed struggle against Austria the Prussian monarchy had practically no prospect of asserting its claim to leadership is at least highly probable, even if it naturally cannot be demonstrated beyond a doubt, no more than can any other of the so-called "historical necessities." European historical research has long been in fundamental agreement on this point. Particularly impressive is the recent work of a Swiss scholar who maintains that Bismarck's German policy was not a matter of personal choice, but was essentially dictated by true reason of state, that is, it represented an amazingly accurate estimate of the only way which could lead to his goal without excessive danger, given the nature of power relationships in Europe and in Germany. Bismarck's phrase about "blood and iron" belongs to those polished aphorisms which he used from time to time to describe a specific situation. They were intended as weapons, but when interpreted as general propositions, they gave rise to very many biased and erroneous opinions about him. On no account is the phrase to be understood as a declaration of a brutal and unscrupulous policy of war and conquest. He never pursued such a policy; indeed, he rejected it completely and unequivocally. But it is admittedly no accident that the phrase has such a shrill and harsh sound. There is a conscious and emphatic belligerence about it, and this belligerence was not without a demonic element.

The great biography of Bismarck by the Anglo-German historian Erich Eyck [*Bismarck: Leben und Werk*, 3 vols., Zurich, 1941–1944] has recently illuminated this demonic element very sharply from the point of view of the older English liberalism associated with Gladstone. It concludes: "Rarely has nature endowed one man with greater riches. But she denied him a sense of right and justice." This verdict has been popularized and vulgarized by mass journalism to imply that for the greatest German statesman might came before right as a matter of principle, that he taught his Germans to share this view, and that he is therefore to be considered the forerunner and pathbreaker of Hitler. In the search for the "roots of National Socialism" in German history Bismarck thus usually appears in a very prominent position beside Frederick the Great, and the modification or destruction of the traditional respect for Bismarck by the German people seems to be one of the most urgent demands of that political reeducation to which our nation is now to be subjected.

No one will have to consider this problem more seriously than the practitioner of German historiography, which, we may venture to say, has been overshadowed for more than half a century by the spirit of Bismarck, which has allowed its political outlook to be largely determined by his ideas, which has with few exceptions believed in the infallibility of at least his foreign policy. As far as his influence in domestic affairs is concerned, there has always been much criticism, and the divisive effects of his activity as organizer and political educator have not gone unnoticed. But how much more profoundly than ever before has his entire lifework come to be questioned, now that the empire which he created has collapsed not only in its monarchical form as in 1918, but in its entirety, and as a result of a brutal policy of might which only too gladly invoked the traditions of Frederick the Great and Bismarck whenever it exalted the demands of power over justice and duty. In such circumstances it could be useful if our attention were directed by Eyck's book toward those aspects of the life of the great exponent of power politics which are particularly alarming to us today, but many of which were formerly overlooked. Among them are his highly biased view of all domestic policy as a constant struggle for power against the party system; the important role of personal hatred and personal ambition in that struggle; his ruthless, at times actually brutal disregard for individuals and legalities not only during the constitutional conflict in Prussia, but also in the period when he was imperial chancellor; his attachment to Junker social prejudices as well as his unmistakable streak of self-seeking; and the limitations in his understanding of domestic policy characteristic of the outlook prevalent east of the Elbe. But there are also instances when the passion of the diplomatic struggle seems to carry him beyond the usual restraints of reason of state, as in the unchivalrously harsh treatment of the city of Frankfurt in 1866, in the advocacy of bloody terror during the struggle against the French guerilla fighters and in the bombardment of Paris, or in the various attempts at intimidation in dealing with the young French Republic until 1875. What today seems to us most serious of all because of its lasting effect is the conscious abuse of political ideas and principles for purely tactical objectives, leading to the spiritual undermining of the great liberal movement which he first opposed and then tried to force into his service, until it degenerated into unprincipled opportunism. By treating the political idealism of the parties as pure doctrinairism, by attempting to transform the German parties of ideology into mere pressure groups, by pitting them against each other in order to assert the power and authority of his monarchical government over them, he destroyed a vast store of good will and a readiness for responsible collaboration, while intensifying economic, social, and religious antagonisms. By his autocratic conduct he also largely suppressed political self-reliance and the willingness to accept responsibility among his ministerial colleagues and among the highest officials of the empire. To speak of a political emasculation of the German middle class would probably be an exaggeration, but certainly after Bismarck's later years the bourgeoisie devoted itself more to economic than political problems. In contrast to Western Europe, parliamentary activity in our country offered to gifted, independent, and ambitious men little opportunity to attain effective power and public recognition. The result was the stagnation of political parties which came to be increasingly controlled by economic pressure groups, the apolitical Philistinism and uncritical loyalty of the petty bourgeois masses, a blind devotion to the state which could easily lead to a blunting of the sense of justice. The effect of Bismarck's rule on the conception of foreign policy accepted by the Germans will have to be discussed separately.

German historiography has no right to deny or prettify all these facts, especially since at times it too was infected with the spirit of "Realpolitik" understood in a Machiavellian sense, and preferred to depict with a certain aesthetic benevolence the demonic qualities in the character of its hero, at least to the extent that these qualities could be used to explain the genius of his political leadership. But there is something else which also belongs among the duties of truthfulness and justice. We must understand and judge each historical phenomenon according to the assumptions of its own time and environment. No political tradition is after all safe against the danger of deterioration. The "realism" of Bismarck is not necessarily refuted by the fact that it served later generations as a justification for deeds of violence. The historian who looks at Bismarck's political methods from English soil, through the eyes of his great opponent Gladstone, may too easily forget the difference of the soil on which he had to take his stand. While Gladstone was the classic, in a certain sense the most extreme champion of English insular and liberal statecraft, Bismarck was the most powerful and determined representative of a Continental, hierarchically organized, actively belligerent great power. As a statesman he was closest to Richelieu. England's liberal empire, in full possession of its economic world hegemony and its naval supremacy, knew armed conflict only on the periphery of its existence, in certain overseas colonial areas. Its foreign policy could assume that all important conflicts of interest may be settled by agreement, by peaceful compromise and deliberation. Bismarck's Prussia was not so fortunate. Here, amid the Great Powers of the Continent, there was no possibility of "splendid isolation," of insular aloofness. In Germany all political hopes of the nation had to be realized through struggle. Instead of calm repose and conciliation, the indispensable virtue of a statesman was strict vigilance and the exertion of all energies. Bismarck himself justified the authoritarian government of his state, of the "constitutional monarchy," by the pressure of an international situation constantly threatened with struggles for power. He argued that the foreign policy of such a state could be successfully conducted only under the completely unrestrained sovereignty of a monarchical government independent of changing parliamentary majorities. German historiography has by and large agreed with him, seeing in his method of government a confirmation of Ranke's thesis concerning the primacy of foreign over domestic policy. According to this thesis the belligerent politics of the Continental state demand an inevitable sacrifice in civic freedom, while the diplomatically more secure existence of the insular state or of the neutral small state makes possible a more easygoing, liberal form of government. Today we see clearly to what exaggerations this doctrine has led: as if the life of a Continental state were constantly threatened; as if there were not even on the Continent many opportunities for a peaceful compromise of conflicting interests without constant resort to arms; as if there were not in a parliamentary state, as the example of France demonstrates, the possibility of a diplomacy which in the tenacious pursuit of power objectives, in its flexibility, in its capacity for swift decision is hardly hindered by parliamentary considerations. Yet it is nevertheless clear that for the great national states of the European continent the laws of life are different from those of the English insular world. Their internal structure as well as their conduct of foreign policy are determined by this difference. Even in England perceptive politicians have long recognized the fact. Philip Kerr, later Lord Lothian, wrote in November 1910 in the introduction to the first number of the journal of the Milner circle, *The Round Table*: "History has taught the Germans the bitter lesson that the citizen can be free only if the state to which he belongs is strong enough to guarantee his freedom."

It is above all from this point of view that Bismarck's war policy must be understood. It did not originate in the passions of a conqueror, adventurer, or militarist, but in the sober *raison d'état* of a military state. The Italian national state was also created only after a long series of armed conflicts, although there the moral authority of monarchical governments was much weaker than in Germany, while revolutionary zeal was much more ardent. Unlike Bismarck, moreover, the liberal statesman Cavour summoned the people against their princes, and enjoyed in addition the moral and military support of a leading foreign power. Even Switzerland and the United States of America did not achieve the development of their federal states into modern national states without major civil wars. The American war of secession of 1861–1865 actually revealed for the first time the horrors and cruelties of waging so-called total war, with its widespread destruction of the country and unprecedented human sacrifices. By comparison the campaign of three weeks which in 1866 decided the exclusion of Austria from the German Confederation seems almost a harmless military parade. It is thus not the conduct of the so-called wars of unification which tends to arouse the moral indignation of foreign observers, but rather their cold, calculated planning far in advance. Yet this is precisely the point at which the historic position of Bismarck in the whole of German and European history becomes most apparent.

He is, in a word, the last great cabinet statesman of European history, a belated Richelieu, to repeat the comparison. Better still, he is a spiritual descendant of Frederick the Great in a completely altered world. He is therefore a profoundly lonely figure, alien to his time. The European cabinets of the seventeenth and eighteenth century waged their wars in accordance with a sober calculation of the power interests of the state, in conscious contrast to the moral and religious passions which had been aroused during the age of religious wars and which had made warfare so bitter and cruel. Bismarck conducted his wars in exactly this fashion, for reason of state pure and simple, in conscious rejection of that incitement of national passion without which no European since the French Revolution can any longer conceive a true war. For him war was in no sense a crusade either for the cause of God or of the nation, but simply a struggle of political forces to determine the superior power. He therefore needed neither the moral depreciation of his opponent nor any sort of self-glorification and self-righteousness. The simple realization that there were conflicting power interests which could no longer be reconciled in a peaceful way was enough. In this sense morality and politics were in his thought sharply separated from each other, whereas generally in the period since the French

Revolution every political conflict tends toward "total" antagonism, that is, not only toward political hostility, but also toward the moral destruction of the opponent as an "enemy." For without such an arousal of feeling and passion a modern nation can no longer be led into war. What an artificial display of moral indignation and political conviction did the Western powers need in order to initiate the greatest cabinet war of the nineteenth century, the Crimean War against Russia. Even Bismarck could not outwardly dispense with it altogether, as the coming of the Franco-Prussian War shows. But in the Prussian monarchy the army was so strictly disciplined and so trained in apolitical loyalty to the throne, that he could undertake the "fratricidal war" of 1866 as a pure cabinet war, against the public opinion of all of Germany, even against the secret aversion of the Prussian chief of the general staff. And how free of moral resentment he himself was is clearly shown by his hard struggle with King William at the end of this cabinet war.

It should be thus quite apparent what a gulf separates Bismarck from a modern nationalist and adventurer like Adolf Hitler. Apart from the vast difference in their intellectual endowment and human quality, there is the distance separating two centuries of European history. Precisely that which characterizes the destroyer of Bismarck's empire and which is the real secret of his meteoric rise was completely alien to the founder of that empire: the fanaticism of national passion which depends upon the blind frenzy of the masses and knows so well how to arouse it. And precisely that which Hitler lacked completely, so that like a man possessed he staggered into the abyss and dragged his nation down with him, was the real secret of Bismarckian statecraft: sober, cool reason of state, unobscured by passion, imposing firm restraints on the exercise of power, pursued with the consummate skill of a born diplomat who knew the great courts of Europe as no other knew them. In view of this difference it is entirely unimportant that both men craved power as all active politicians do, that both were therefore inclined to equate their state with themselves. For the upstart this state was only a tool of the "party," in other words, his own tool. When the end came, the entire nation would and should go down with him. For the prime minister of old Prussia the possession of power was ultimately an opportunity to serve others.

Franz Schnabel

Old Means and Old Purposes

When the reign of National Socialism finally came to an end amid the devastation of World War II, Gerhard Ritter and Franz Schnabel emerged as leaders of the postwar German historians. Whereas the former emphasized the continuing validity of national tradition, the latter became the spokesman for a cautious revisionism. Schnabel had established himself as a scholar of the first rank with the publication of his masterly history of Germany in the nineteenth century. But the Third Reich forced him into retirement from which he did not emerge until 1945, when he accepted the chair of modern history at the University of Munich. While recognizing Bismarck's great gifts, he criticized the nationalist solution of the unification problem.

We may correctly speak of Bismarck's being "misunderstood" nowadays in the sense that his work and activity have been viewed apart from their connection with the previous system of states and its political conceptions. Bismarck's conduct was dictated by a line which traced back to Frederick the Great, Richelieu, Gustavus Adolphus and Maurice de Saxe. They all contributed to the destruction of Western unity, to the establishment of sovereign states, and to their mighty expansion by conquest, treaty-breaking and violence against the weak. For a long time, Bismarck merely put modern nationalism to his own uses. He was, first and foremost, the managing director of a state which played the role of a great power in the European state system of five great powers and many smaller powers; as yet, Prussia was not "saturated" within this state system. Once he said that Prussia wore too heavy armor for her small body. It is an image which corresponds to the old political thinking. Bismarck did not learn the new metaphors of nationalism. He was concerned with the interests of the state, with the state as a rational system of analysis

Source: From Franz Schnabel, "The Bismarck Problem," in Hans Kohn, ed., *German History: Some New German Views* (Boston: Beacon Press and George Allen & Unwin Ltd., 1954), pp. 82–89, 92–93.

and action. Hence he remained strange to the voluntarisms of the period of national states and democracy. The program and slogans of nationalism — natural living space, historical borders, assimilation and national will — which derived in part from the French Revolution and for the rest from German romanticism, were widespread among the liberals in the sixties and seventies, and were already being fully acted upon among the Eastern European peoples. Bismarck did not heed any of these slogans; he disregarded this program. Even when he annexed Alsace and Lorraine, military considerations were paramount in his mind. He belonged to the system of states as it had been, when states looked out for themselves and wished to please only themselves, when the interests of the state were all that was at stake and the interests of the people were only of secondary concern. He brought two new great powers, Prussia-Germany and Sardinia-Italy into the old European state system. As a result, he transformed the "European concert." The forces which later put an axe to the entire historical state structure had been in being for a long time, and Bismarck had to reckon with them. But he still hoped to be able to bring them under control.

The methods used by Bismarck therefore derived from the old policy of European governments. It saw in power the proper purpose of the state. It had extricated the states from the medieval bonds of universalism, and involved them in the struggle for hegemony or balance of power. Modern nationalism was a new form of this spirit of separatism. Therefore, Bismarck had been able to make it his ally; with it he brought new elements of power into the battle array. He saw that, as a result, Europe would have to make rapid progress toward ruin. But he thought that the traditional state system, in whose categories he thought and acted, was strong. It would survive the profound contradiction which he brought about when he created a Prussian-German national state in Central Europe and at the same time tried to protect and preserve the pure dynastic states against the nationalities in Eastern Europe. For historical judgment this question is therefore clearly crucial: was there, in fact, any chance in Bismarck's time of giving up the free competition of interests? It would have made superfluous the old methods by which affairs had been conducted until then. Could there have been established as a consequence, cooperative life of men and peoples upon Christian principles, or at least a system corresponding to these principles more closely than the previous system? It cannot be maintained that Bismarck did not dare to set himself against his time. He thrust himself very energetically athwart the liberal and democratic movement, which certainly belonged to the advancing forces of the time, and hindered their development. On the other hand, the Frederician tradition in which he grew up was no longer a vital force at that instant; it regained its power during Bismarck's lifetime and mainly by his exertions. The choice was up to him. Would he remain under the spell of the old diplomacy and adopt in consequence its theory that the compact national state was the necessary form in which the nations could achieve their fulfillment? In that case, to be consistent, he would have had to "write off" the Habsburg monarchy. But he did not. Or, would he feel himself called upon to seek new paths in order to satisfy the nations of Central and Eastern European territories into a jumble of lands like the Balkans?

A statesman who did not accept the compact national state certainly had no lack of allies and forces at his disposal. Everywhere the majority of peoples still adhered to their hereditary princes. Of course, a small ducal state with a Serene Highness at its head no longer furnished an adequate area in which to function. But numerous connections had by then been set up between countries. Extension of the Prussian customs union (*Zollverein*) was possible; it was wholly justified by economic conditions, and only the school of the old diplomacy thwarted its achievement. Above all, however, the German Confederation could have been further developed. After the events of 1848 and 1849, the governments, including that of Prussia before Bismarck came upon the scene, were ready. Moreover, the question whether the vital rights of the nation could not be satisfied in this way as well, still remained completely open. The Danubian monarchy of the Habsburgs was not to be saved. It could break apart into national states. There would be frightful struggles especially in territories of mixed national composition. Or the Habsburg realms could be transformed into a Central European federation of nations, each living its own life again under new constitutional arrangements. In Vienna, as in Berlin, the decision had not yet been taken. Despite 1848–1849, the awakening of the nationalities in Eastern Europe had only begun. They took what they could use and were as yet not out of control. Only in the eighties did radicalism finally break through to them as a consequence of the system of 1866. There had been a time when national hatred between Englishmen and Scotsmen was elemental and fierce, yet it had been buried. To be sure, with the Irish this did not come successfully to pass. The examples of the United States and France were beyond contradiction. The nationalities were also set in motion by the doctrines of German romanticism. But after 1849 there was everywhere very great fear of Russia, and Pan-Slavism was still just something happening within literary romanticism. There was a profound basis in the course of modern history for the endeavor of all the peoples of Europe to develop, each in its own way, toward the goal of forming its own state. They were still in the habit of calling in a king from old dynasties, from foreign lands. Personal union was found to be a satisfactory solution, and there were many other such solutions. The demand for a compact national organism came only from a few parties, and was chiefly a product of the scholars. Furthermore, if a statesman knew world conditions, he could not help but see the problems of the Continent more profoundly than could Bismarck, whose policy was limited to the Continent. He could not escape the deep contradiction which cleaved apart the entire age: When nationalism had free course, it led to a dismemberment of Europe; at the same time, the technology of communications, which in the shape of the locomotive had already outrun the small states and was a pacemaker for the nation and for democracy, was advancing. It was overcoming distance ever more quickly and thereby compelling a changeover to world communications and a world economy.

There was, therefore, a good basis in the actual conditions for federal union of the Central and Eastern European peoples. The new arrangement could be developed upon an existing foundation with existing forces and energies. Any other goal signified an extension of the revolutionary policy which had already shaken Europe for so long a period of time. The revolutionary forces at various times had brought to the forefront one or another artificial power-state. These forces now included as well the active portion of the urban bourgeoisie which, as Ranke said at the time, dreamed that they could "construct out of their wits" their fatherland. Some constructed a *kleindeutsch* monarchy, others a *grossdeutsch* centralized republic. But the time when Bismarck was preparing and carrying through his work was also filled with plans tied to existing reality. Constantin Frantz was only the most active and the intellectually most important of those who told Bismarck that the security which the German people so urgently required when future world decisions would be made, could not be guaranteed by means of the isolated national state, and by the combination of alliances which Bismarck with great skill formed anew time and again. It should not be said, therefore, that the conceptions of a federative Europe were mere literature. The very *kleindeutsch* doctrine which came so conveniently to Bismarck's hand, had been elaborated in scholars' studies. And it is not correct either to say that the conception of a Central European federation of national states was premature, that it would only be justified when the nations would come to fear their own likeness unto God and saw themselves placed between two rising world powers. The moment quickly passed during which, as fate would have it, serious discussion of such a federation of Europe was possible. No one talked any more of union of the nations of Central and Eastern Europe, or of a Europe existing upon the basis of its own strength. Only in Bismarck's time could this idea have been carried out and the self-laceration of the nations prevented. It was already obvious that the appearance of Russia in Central Europe, which anyone could see by 1849, was a world event of incalculable consequences. It necessarily opened up a new world epoch, with new methods in diplomacy and a new European attitude.

Here one may well object that no serious opponent of Bismarck, able to carry through such a policy, came forward. Controversial historiography, though it has its rights like any other, should never lose from view the fact that Germany at that time had lived for many centuries in political decrepitude. The German Confederation did indeed constitute a new beginning, but it was not yet a living political organism. Metternich, on whom rests responsibility for the three decades of German history from 1815 to 1848, permitted political life in the individual states to go farther. It was certainly of great value that the German people got the habit of acting in accordance with free political forms in the legislatures of south and central German states. But 1848 was the penalty paid because only those who supported the national state solutions had set programs. Austria's leadership in fact signified stagnation and reaction. Bismarck was the only statesman who took energetic action; he opened the valve to release the accumulated energies. An immense conflict in German life now broke out again, to be decided once and for all — on the one side the House of Habsburg, which for centuries had found its profit in maintaining things as they were; and on the other Frederician policy brought back to life! The liberals joined Bismarck's camp when he began to prove successful. The more they had previously placed their hopes upon Prussia and the Prussian monarchy, while rejecting Prussian methods, the longer was their resistance. The power of the personal factor in history was displayed with particular vigor in this regard. Yet the fact remains that the organization of Germany permitted of no delay, and that, in any event, whenever Austria would prove hesitant, Prussia would act.

Although Bismarck was therefore able to drive German history along the road to disaster, clearly he did not shoulder sole responsibility. It was borne equally by those other German forces still in existence at the time which did not set up a rival leader of equal stature. He was far superior to his liberal adversaries, like Roggenbach and Bennigsen, who wished to give a different constitution to the national state. One looks in vain in Prussia for a statesman of rank who would have been able to carry on the policy of peaceful dualism. In the middle-sized states there were no German princes as active on the *grossdeutsch*, federalist side as the Grand Duke of Baden was in the *kleindeutsch*, liberal camp; none was so popular as Duke Ernst of Gotha, the "sharpshooter Duke." Even Windthorst did not have his king's support; he was only an administrative minister and, when the hour of decision drew near, had once more been dropped from the ministry of state. In any case, we must look into the actual capacity of Count Beust as a statesman who, in the years of the foundation of the Reich, was Bismarck's leading opponent. Did he lose out to Bismarck because the Prussian statesman took a course of action which did not look far into the future, and so was much simpler and easier to follow? Because Bismarck opened the way for his policy, and followed it with no scruples of conscience, brushing aside violently considerations of law and justice? But it is still very doubtful whether the governing caste of the old Austrian monarchy would have permitted any statesman to carry through fundamental reorganization. It is true, of course, that Count Julius Andrassy, who was certainly a statesman of scope, received a free hand for a foreign policy which differed very greatly from that previously in effect. The nationalities brought forth personalities like Deák, who wished to guide nationalism along orderly channels. But, while Bismarck gave the example and brought on the decision, it was the Magyars who none the less were the essential driving force. The Czechs, on the contrary, hesitated for a while. At that time, there were important intellectuals among them. For a long time they endeavored to achieve peaceful reorganization of the monarchy, they kept in sight the danger threatening them from the east. But, for much too long, the answer which was given in Vienna, and in Berlin as well, was that things would not be changed under any circumstances. Archduke Franz Ferdinand came much too late. But it is often true in history that when the political turn of affairs is propitious, it brings forth the statesman who is needed. Who will deny that there were still many chances of development which even the Austrian court could not reject in the long run? It was Bismarck who destroyed these prospects. It may reasonably be doubted that, in the long run, such a federal state would have been able to provide security against the overwhelming growth of Russia. But the fact remains that there were forces in Central Europe which could have been spared and combined, which the rivalries and competition of the national state system used up at an enormous rate. Because of his origin and character, Bismarck was never able to take this path; in fact, as a result, he gave an intensely personal direction to the history of Germany and Europe. The situation which he faced at the start of his career was that the peoples of Europe were attacking the work of the Congress of Vienna; they wished once more to destroy it. But the decision was his that this would come about only by way of annexations and militarism, and that the nations had to adopt the capitalist system in self-preservation. Thus, very much against his will, he did most to bring about the dissolution of Central and Eastern Europe into purely independent national states.

We now know the steps by which this disaster, as we must call it today, was brought about. From the very first day of his official activity, Bismarck with fiery zeal loosened the ties with Austria, forced it out of Germany, abandoned it to the struggle of nationalities within it and created the Prussian-German state which could maintain itself only by alternating alliances with other power-states in the fashion of the old political system. The enormity of the enduring alliance with Russia against Austria was in itself a demonstration of the extent to which the new empire was totally incorporated into the great power system, entirely abandoned to the uncertain play of forces between the powers, and remaining wholly dependent upon one man's virtuosity. The many eulogists of Bismarck among German historians have praised to the highest his ostensible moderation in making the armistice with Austria at Nikolsburg in 1866; because it prevented the collapse of Austria at that moment, the later national radicalism of all nationalities found cause to regret it. In truth there is nothing in it either to be praised or blamed. The whole system of 1866, this last and much extolled "masterpiece" of the old style, resulted at once in the decline of the Habsburg Empire. Thus it was the cause of the isolation and downfall of the Bismarckian Empire as well. The nationalities were in fact encouraged by the success of the German movement. They took advantage of the weaknesses of the monarchy which had been defeated on the battlefield. As soon as the nationalities lay free and unprotected along the Russian border, Central Europe in turn could no longer maintain its own position. The old statecraft was utterly confounded. . . .

By destiny and tendency Bismarck's profession became the modern political system of reason of state and embattled interests. He found joy in this activity. He considered that territorial compactness and the independence of modern great states, which recognize legal order among themselves only in the shape of alternating alliances, constituted not merely a valuable, but in fact a final achievement of civilization. In order to safeguard and to extend this system of state power, he promoted the welfare of the people, though wholly in the spirit of the old statecraft, and was convinced that only a power-state could guarantee happiness and prosperity. Since the situation in which he found himself demanded his active intervention, he was not squeamish in the choice of his means and did not seek farther afield after new, better ways. He took for granted the state world in which he lived, and believed that Prussia was called upon to achieve something valuable in this system. He considered a compact state organism in the heart of Europe to be a higher form of life than a federation of states carried to another stage of development. There were many esteemed thinkers who, though they had their doubts, still sought to justify the statesman and to encourage him in this course. Powerful intellectual currents of the time assisted in this change. They led farther and farther away from the conception of law and from Christianity. But the statesman did not wholly realize what an alliance he was accepting. The life work which he built was certainly not profoundly thought out, but one would do injustice to its master if one were to forget that the spiritual life of his time had in general lost all direction, that numerous and contradictory standpoints were represented with scholarship of equal breadth and with equal impressiveness, and that it was extremely difficult for the statesman to reach a position of fixity and validity. The creator of the second German Empire remained entirely gripped by the contradictions of his age. He made shift with the old means and the old purposes. This had never before led to enduring order; now the passions were all aroused as well. Bismarck took part in this release from control. He believed that he could utilize the new impulsion to be found in the crowd for the power of his state, and at the same time limit it by a rational system called reason of state. He did not come to a realization that in a world of such confusions there are tasks which go far beyond the state, and that it was becoming extremely necessary to bring the state back to its original purpose, to help establish the good, the right, the higher order. His position remained that the statesman's task consisted in nothing more than development of the state. Were there statesmen who saw farther than he? We cannot be sure. But he did become the first man of his time. Upon him depended essentially the further course of events. In history, however, only those forces are preserved which devote themselves to world historic goals. And the only standard by which peoples and civilizations can be measured and differentiated is whether a belief in a higher world order lives on in them.

G. P. Gooch

The Divorce of Politics from Morals

George Peabody Gooch was blessed with a remarkable longevity that so
many European historians seem to enjoy. He continued until his nine-
ties to combine good scholarship with good writing as felicitously as
ever. In the course of his long career he had proved himself a gifted
lecturer and had sat in the House of Commons with the Liberals. But
his claim to fame rests most securely on the numerous works of history
published over more than half a century. While he was at home in many
periods and many nations, his greatest interest was modern Germany.
In his article "Bismarck's Legacy" Gooch summarized a lifetime of
study of the Iron Chancellor.

The lessons of Bismarck's political testament and unique career fall
into two classes: those which concern statesmen of all times, and
those specifically addressed to his own countrymen. The most important in the first category is enshrined in his celebrated aphorism:
"Politics are the art of the possible," by which he meant the meticulous adjustment of ends to means. *Qui trop embrasse mal étreint.*
Though nothing appears so obvious as the need for horse sense on
the stony paths of *haute politique,* no maxim has proved more difficult to apply by those who scale the giddy summits of power. The
difference between practicable aims and *Caesarenwahnsin* was
sharply illustrated by the careers of Frederick the Great and Napoleon. The former staked his fortunes on the seizure of Silesia, which
events were to prove within his capacity to accomplish and retain.
Though he cherished and fulfilled other territorial ambitions, he
never dreamed of fighting for them. Napoleon, on the other hand,
intoxicated by his early victories in Italy, followed his delusive star
and ended at St. Helena. The contrasted experiences of Bismarck

Source: G. P. Gooch, "Bismarck's Legacy," reprinted by permission of *Foreign Affairs,*
30 (1952), pp. 527–530. Copyright 1952 by the Council on Foreign Relations, Inc.

and Hitler tell a similar tale. The former set out with a bold but limited resolve and when he reached his goal he sheathed the sword. It was not a case of the Prussian eagle borrowing the silky plumes of a dove, but a clear-eyed perception that there were limits to the strength of the Reich. Preventive wars he repudiated on the ground that no mortal could read the cards of Providence. The outstanding figure of the era of nationalism was neither an imperialist, for he never desired to impose German rule on alien races, nor a Pan-German, since he never aspired to bring all Germans into one fold. So long as he remained at the helm it could not be seriously argued that the new Reich had misused its strength. Hitler, on the other hand, neurotic, inexperienced, and trusting to his intuitions, was spurred forward by ambition as insatiable as that of Napoleon, and even before his appointment as chancellor he confided to Rauschning his fantastic dreams. Like Napoleon he never — in Byron's words — learned "that tempted fate will leave the loftiest star."

From this general principle of limiting risks stemmed a salutary exhortation to his countrymen, whose recurring temptation, located at the center of the European chessboard without natural frontiers, has been to hit out in all directions. During the medieval *Kaiserzeit* it was an urge to the south, in the twentieth century the call of East and West. A weak and divided Germany has always been a tempting bait to greedy neighbors, a united and powerful Germany a potential threat. Though Bismarck solemnly adjured her rulers to avoid the simultaneous estrangement of East and West, the warning was in vain. In that well-organized state, it has been remarked, there was anarchy at the top. While Tirpitz, bent on challenging Britain's naval predominance, urged the covering of the German flank through an understanding with Russia, Bethmann advocated friendly relations with England as a condition of forward moves in the Middle East. Both policies had their advantages and their risks, and a choice should have been made between them, but there was no Bismarck to make it. Had he revisited the scenes of his triumphs in the opening decade of the twentieth century, he would have been appalled by the transformation of a friendly England and a neutral Russia into potential foes. Had he returned for a second time at the close of the second decade, he would have pointed in grief and anger to the result of a policy of uninsurable risks. Like the Emperor Augustus after the defeat of Varus in the battle of the

Teutoburger Wald, he might have murmured: "Give me back my legions."

Statesmen can learn much of their trade in Bismarck's school but not the whole. *Raison d'état* is a polite name for an ugly thing — the divorce of politics from morals. This gospel of anarchy, formulated though not invented by Machiavelli, has been practiced, if not always professed, by men of all races, all creeds, by good and bad alike. "If I see my opportunity," exclaimed Frederick the Great when the sudden death of the Emperor Charles VI opened the road to Breslau, "shall I not take it?" Napoleon dismissed as *idéologues* men who, as he believed, refused to look facts in the face. In the latter half of the nineteenth century Cavour and Bismarck played the familiar game with complete lack of moral scruple and with consummate skill. "If we did for ourselves what we do for our country," remarked the maker of United Italy, "what rascals we should be." Among the most successful of his stratagems was the dispatch of a beautiful countess to win the support of Napoleon III in expelling the Austrians from Lombardy. Though Bismarck stressed the importance of *imponderabilia*, when the right hour struck he acted and let the world say what it liked. It is an error to regard Prussia as more of an aggressor than Piedmont and Bismarck as morally inferior to Cavour. It was not till the shattering experience of the First World War revealed the insufficiency of the sovereign state in an increasingly interdependent world that Woodrow Wilson, General Smuts, Lord Cecil and other practical idealists launched a crusade for a system which seemed to promise less tragic results.

A second weakness in Bismarckian statesmanship was his neglect to train his countrymen for self-government. His grant of adult male suffrage suggested confidence in their wisdom and patriotism; but the Reichstag proved — and was intended to prove — little more than a fig-leaf, to use Liebknecht's drastic expression, to cover the nakedness of autocracy. That the power of the purse might have been put to better use is true enough, but the core of the constitution was the retention of final decisions in nonelective hands. A further bar to the democratization of Germany was the maintenance of the three-class voting system invented by Frederick William IV for Prussia, which contained two-thirds of the population of the Reich and in which the rapidly growing army of urban workers did not count. So obsessed was Bismarck by the principle of undivided responsibility that, though he was prepared to admit to office Bennigsen, the trusty leader of the National Liberals, he declined the request to bring two of his parliamentary colleagues with him, and the project of broadening the basis of government was dropped. When the Hohenzollern Empire fell with a crash in 1918 the problems of Weimar Germany had to be faced by amateurs.

It was not solely the fault of the chancellor, for there was little demand for parliamentary government except among the Socialists and the Radicals. Collaboration worked well enough in south Germany, but the emperor, the army chief, the Junkers and the great industrialists of the Rhineland objected to entrusting the proletariat with a substantial share of power. Conservative historians such as Hans Delbrück and Adalbert Wahl regarded the Bismarckian constitution as a model blending of popular representation with an irremovable executive, thus ensuring continuity in foreign policy and national defense. Liberal scholars, on the other hand, such as Ziekursch and Erich Eyck, censure him for ignoring the world-wide demand for parliamentary government. He could not live forever, and no other superman was in sight. Officials nominated or dominated by the ruler are as liable to make mistakes as ministers responsible to Parliament.

Bismarck bequeathed to his grateful countrymen a superb inheritance: a nation-state, a Triple Alliance to ensure its safety, a federal constitution which satisfied the rulers of the component states, the beginnings of social security, colonial territory, and a prestige unknown since the Emperor Barbarossa. Almost all these assets were thrown away by the shortsighted successors who forgot that politics are the art of the possible. It is one of the ironies of history that his most enduring monument should be a book which would never have been written but for the accident of his dismissal. The action of a young ruler, so hotly resented by his victim, unwittingly set the seal on his immeasurable renown.

Bismarck spoke disdainfully of "Professor Gladstone," but are the practitioners of Realpolitik as much wiser as they believe? Their weakness is to think too much of immediate returns and too little of the long-range results of their hammer strokes. Vast and splendid as was his intellect, he could see nothing and imagine nothing beyond the sovereign state pursuing exclusively its own supposed interests. Europe was only a geographical expression. The vision of an organized world, an international order resting on a willing partnership of self-governing national units, was beyond his ken. The presupposition of all profitable political and economic planning is a firm grasp of the unity of civilization. To the shaping of the human spirit for that supreme adventure of the human spirit he contributed nothing. He labored exclusively for his countrymen — first for Prussia and later for a Prussianized Reich — and was satisfied with their applause. In a word, he dates, for we have learned by bitter experience that nationalism is not enough. Yet the twentieth century will have little right to throw stones at the nineteenth until all the Great Powers begin to operate a system more conducive to human welfare than that which the Iron Chancellor practiced and preached.

Suggestions for Additional Reading

The historical literature on Bismarck is enormous. In Germany only Luther and Goethe have inspired a comparable volume of writing, while outside Central Europe no one can compete with the Iron Chancellor except Napoleon and Lincoln. An exhaustive list of books and articles dealing with his life and times has never been compiled. It is probably an impossible task. But a comprehensive collection of older titles appears in the standard bibliographical work on the history of Germany: F. C. Dahlmann and Georg Waitz, eds., *Quellenkunde der deutschen Geschichte,* 9th ed., 2 vols (Leipzig, 1931), 1:870–897, 940–952. It cites well over two thousand publications. Some of the important works appearing since then are listed in the short but very useful book by Walter Bussmann, *Das Zeitalter Bismarcks* (Konstanz, 1956), pp. 251–274, which constitutes volume three, part two, of Otto Brandt, Arnold Oskar Meyer, and Leo Just, eds., *Handbuch der deutschen Geschichte,* 4 vols. (Marburg, Darmstadt, and Konstanz, 1952–1959), and in the second volume of Lothar Gall's biography, pp. 251–270. The sheer bulk of Bismarckian scholarship can be gauged from the fact that in Maximilian von Hagen, *Das Bismarckbild in der Literatur der Gegenwart* (Berlin, 1929), which describes the writings published in the twelve years from 1915 to 1927, there are accounts of more than a hundred and fifty works. And yet the author explains apologetically that he has been able to deal only with the more important titles.

While the German bibliographical publications are indispensable to the trained scholar, their effect on the beginner is unpredictable. It takes courage to face a list of hundreds of books in a foreign language, and it would perhaps be best if neophytes did not expose themselves right at the outset to what could prove an intimidating experience. There are fortunately several excellent accounts in English of the Bismarck literature. G. P. Gooch, "The Study of Bismarck," in his *Studies in German History* (London, 1948), pp. 300–341, is sure to stimulate readers' interest. Scholarly, urbane, and perceptive, it is a model essay on bibliography. For a much briefer but still serviceable description, see G. F. Howe, G. C. Boyce, T. R. S. Broughton, et al., eds., *The American Historical Association's Guide to Historical Literature* (New York, 1961), pp. 555–557. Lawrence D. Steefel, who wrote the standard work on the diplomacy of the

Danish War of 1864, published an article on the Bismarckian literature of the 1920s entitled simply "Bismarck," *Journal of Modern History* 2 (1930): 74-95. For some of the works published after World War II, there are three useful critical reviews easily available to American readers. Andreas Dorpalen, "The German Historians and Bismarck," *Review of Politics* 15 (1953): 53-67, is the most comprehensive. As the title suggests, Hans Kohn, "Rethinking Recent German History," ibid. 14 (1952): 325-345, does not deal with the Bismarck problem exclusively, but it devotes a good deal of attention to the issues raised by the unification of Germany. Finally, Otto Pflanze in the early part of his article on "Bismarck and German Nationalism," *American Historical Review* 60 (1955): 548-566, describes some major interpretations of the Iron Chancellor.

The most important part of the Bismarck literature is what he himself wrote and said. The publication of his speeches and letters began while he was still alive, but there was no systematic collection of his various writings until the appearance of *Die gesammelten Werke* (15 vols. in 19, Berlin, 1924-1935). This great work of painstaking scholarship contains political polemics, conversations, addresses, letters, and memoirs. Yet despite its vast scope it is not complete, and should be supplemented with other compilations of Bismarck materials. For his speeches, for example, there is Horst Kohl, ed., *Die politischen Reden des Fürsten Bismarck*, 14 vols. (Stuttgart and Berlin, 1892-1905); for his diplomacy after the formation of the German Empire there are the first six volumes of Johannes Lepsius, Albrecht Mendelssohn Bartholdy, and Friedrich Thimme, eds., *Die grosse Politik der europäischen Kabinette, 1871-1914: Sammlung der diplomatischen Akten des Auswärtigen Amtes* (40 vols. in 54, Berlin, 1922-1927); and for his private talks there is Heinrich von Poschinger, *Fürst Bismarck und die Parlamentarier*, 3 vols. (Breslau, 1894-1896). Hans Rothfels has edited an excellent one-volume collection of his writings under the title *Otto von Bismarck: Deutscher Staat* (Munich, 1925), which constitutes volume twenty-one of the series *Der deutsche Staatsgedanke*. The introduction to this book, by the way, provides a thoughtful analysis of its protagonist's political philosophy.

While it would be futile to attempt serious research in the Bismarckian period without a good reading knowledge of German, the amount of material available in English is not inconsiderable.

The memoirs were translated under the title *Bismarck: The Man and the Statesman*, 2 vols. (New York and London, 1899); some of the diplomatic writings from *Die grosse Politik* appear in the first volume of E. T. S. Dugdale, ed., *German Diplomatic Documents, 1871–1914*, 4 vols. (London, 1928–1931); the three solid volumes of the *Tischgespräche* have been reduced to one in Charles Lowe, ed., *Bismarck's Table Talk* (London, 1895); and some of the important collections of letters were published as *The Correspondence of William I and Bismarck*, 2 vols. (New York, 1903), and *The Love Letters of Bismarck* (New York and London, 1901). American readers can thus obtain in their native language a firsthand acquaintance with the Iron Chancellor.

Next in importance to Bismarck's public and private papers are the writings of those who worked with him during his thirty years as the leading statesman of Germany. The vast literature of reminiscences, however, must be handled with care. The number of people who met the Iron Chancellor in one capacity or another was huge, and many of them were eager to bask in the reflected glory of his name. Moritz Busch, Bismarck's propagandist and confidant, published his diary in an English translation immediately after the statesman's death under the title *Bismarck: Some Secret Pages of His History*, 2 vols. (New York, 1898). The German edition in a somewhat censored form appeared a year later as *Tagebuchblätter*, 3 vols. (Leipzig, 1899). Robert Lucius von Ballhausen was a prominent politician and minister of agriculture in the later years of the reign of William I. His *Bismarck-Erinnerungen* (Stuttgart, 1920) presents an impressive and detailed portrait of the chancellor. Robert von Keudell knew the Bismarck family intimately, so that his *Fürst und Fürstin Bismarck: Erinnerungen aus den Jahren 1846–1872* (Berlin and Stuttgart, 1901) is a revealing account of the private life as well as the political activity of its hero during the struggle for national unification. Some of the most valuable memoirs were written by officials whose task it was to execute the chancellor's diplomatic designs. The diaries of Prince Chlodwig zu Hohenlohe-Schillingsfürst, *Denkwürdigkeiten*, 2 vols. (Stuttgart and Leipzig, 1906), are of major significance. They have appeared in English as *Memoirs of Prince Chlodwig of Hohenlohe-Schillingsfuerst*, 2 vols. (New York, 1906). General Hans Lothar von Schweinitz, who served under Bismarck as his country's ambassador to Austria and Russia, made important disclosures about the statecraft of his chief in *Denkwürdigkeiten des Botschafters General v. Schweinitz,* 2 vols. (Berlin, 1927). And Count Alfred von Waldersee in his recollections edited by H. O. Meisner as *Denkwürdigkeiten des General-Feldmarschalls Alfred Grafen von Waldersee,* 3 vols. (Stuttgart and Berlin, 1922–1923) throws light on the Iron Chancellor's last years in power.

The biographies of Bismarck continue to multiply, as both critics and defenders reinterpret his career in the light of subsequent history. Selections from Erich Marcks, A. J. P. Taylor, Otto Pflanze, Erich Eyck, and Lothar Gall appear in this book. But there are several other lives of the Iron Chancellor that ought not to be overlooked. Max Lenz, *Geschichte Bismarck* (Leipzig, 1902) is one of the earliest biographical studies, but it can still be read with profit. For the period of the constitutional conflict and the wars of unification there is the account in English by James Wycliffe Headlam, *Bismarck and the Foundation of the German Empire* (New York, 1899). The best French biography remains Paul Matter, *Bismarck et son temps,* 3 vols. (Paris, 1905–1908). Written before World War I, these works accepted the state that Bismarck had created as viable and sound. Then came the collapse of the German Empire, which produced a revisionist school of Bismarckian scholarship. Such adverse interpretations as Karl Scheffler, *Bismarck: Eine Studie* (Leipzig, 1919), Hermann Kantorowicz, *Bismarcks Schatten* (Freiburg, 1921), and Friedrich Wilhelm Foerster, *Bismarcks Werk im Licht der föderalistischen Kritik* (Ludwigsburg, 1921) contended that the Iron Chancellor was ultimately responsible for the tragedy that had befallen his country, since the ends as well as the means of his diplomacy were bound to lead to disaster. The argument, however, failed to persuade many readers. The prevailing view was expressed in Otto Hammann, *Der missverstandne Bismarck: Zwanzig Jahre deutscher Weltpolitik* (Berlin, 1921), which maintained that it was not Bismarck but his inept successors who must bear the blame for Germany's ruin. Only since World War II has there been among scholars a consistently critical attitude toward Bismarck, although he still has his champions in historians like Arnold Oskar Meyer, *Bismarck: Der Mensch und der Staatsmann* (Stuttgart, 1949), and the more restrained Wilhelm Mommisen, *Bismarck: Ein politisches Lebensbild* (Munich, 1959).

An understanding of Bismarck's life necessarily depends on an understanding of his time. The activities of the statesman must be seen in their proper milieu, so that a study of political and economic history ought to supplement the reading of biographical accounts. On the rise of the movement for national unification in Germany from the War of Liberation to the Franco-Prussian War there is still the substantial opus of Adolphus William Ward, *Germany, 1815– 1890*, 3 vols. (Cambridge, 1916–1918). It is largely overshadowed, however, by two other major works that are no less scholarly and much more penetrating: Erich Brandenburg, *Die Reichsgründung*, 2 vols. (Leipzig, 1916), and Erich Marcks, *Der Aufstieg des Reiches: Deutsche Geschichte von 1807–1871/78*, 2 vols. (Stuttgart, 1936). Both agree that the ultimate objectives of Bismarckian statecraft were not only sound but necessary. For the German Empire, William Harbutt Dawson holds up surprisingly well. But his book is no substitute for the volumes of Johannes Ziekursch and Adalbert Wahl. The former's history, openly critical of the chancellor's autocratic tendencies, is probably the best overall treatment of the period. Yet on many points it should be checked with the latter's *Deutsche Geschichte von der Reichsgründung bis zum Ausbruch des Weltkriegs (1871 bis 1914)*, 4 vols. (Stuttgart, 1926–1936), a spirited defense of Bismarck's political philosophy written from a conservative point of view. While German historians have generally avoided any out-and-out condemnation of the unifier of their country, foreign scholars have felt no similar reticence. The Englishman A. J. P. Taylor, *The Course of German History* (New York, 1946), the American Koppel S. Pinson, *Modern Germany* (New York, 1954), and the Frenchman Edmond Vermeil, *L'Allemangne: Essai d'explication* (Paris, 1940), translated as *Germany's Three Reichs* (London, 1945), agree that the Iron Chancellor taught his countrymen to worship power and submit to authority. This is also the conclusion reached by Hajo Holborn in his massive *History of Modern Germany*, 3 vols. (New York, 1959–1969). For the historical background of the German Empire, there are two useful recent works: Thomas Nipperdey, *Deutsche Geschichte, 1800–1866: Bürgerwelt und starker Staat* (Munich, 1983), and James J. Sheehan, *German History, 1770–1866* (Oxford and New York, 1989). Gordon A. Craig, *Germany, 1866–1945* (New York, 1978), provides a perceptive and informative account of the rise and fall of Bismarck's political creation.